GROWING INTO
A MAN OF GRACE

DARYL JAMES

Wisdom, Prayers, & Life Lessons

ISBN-13: 9798675116508

Unless otherwise noted all scripture quotations are from the King James Version of the Bible. These quotations are often marked KJV.

Take note that in some instances pronouns such as "He" are capitalized when referring to any Three Members of the Holy Trinity, including Father, Son, and Holy Spirit. This is a personal choice to exalt God and acknowledge God even to the extent of grammatical rules.

This book was printed in the United States of America

Editor: Latanya "Epiphany" Richardson
Publisher Epiphany Books
Cover Design: Latanya "Epiphany" Richardson

ACKNOWLEDGEMENTS

First and foremost, I would love to give thanks and praises to Almighty GOD for all he has done. I thank Him for all He's doing and what He's yet to do. Without Him, I am nothing but with Him, I can do all things.

Next, this book is dedicated in loving memory of my wife, Sharon Christine James. She encouraged me, enlightened me, and covered me daily. She loved me unconditionally, saved my life when I was lost and hurt by bringing me back into the love of GOD. With her help I now I take refuge and recognize His blessings on my life every day. She made me a better son, brother, father and man. I am so grateful for all she's done for me. I'll never stop loving her because she never stopped loving me until her last breath. I thank GOD for her, and she will forever remain in my heart.

I'd like to thank my family, Coralita E., Donalda C., Patricia B. for your love and support. I also thank my daughters, Jasmine D, Jessica A. James and Jennifer A. Smith. I thank you all for being the best daughters a father could ever ask for.

To the man who gave me my surname and the man with my surname as his middle name. My father, the late Donald F. James, went on to glory, God rest his soul.

To my father in law, Willie J. Nicklow, you definitely stepped up to the plate and filled the void that my father left. Along with James R. Terry, Treacy M. Preer and the late Peggy A. Nicklow thank you all for accepting me and allowing me to be part of the family.

I thank my Impact Church family for being a great church and giving me grace to grow. To Bishop De'Andre Salter aka Pastor D. May God continue to strengthen and lengthen your life and use you for His glory. I love you and support you brother because I want to be one of the first on that bus. I appreciate you and your lovely wife, Lady Terri Jones Salter for your patience, love, understanding, friendship and fellowship.

Vincent Booker who we all affectionately call, Deac, short for Deacon Booker. Shout out to Deac, appreciate you from the bottom of my heart. Thanks for being the brother I always wanted.

Thank you to all my extended families and friends. Your contributions to my growth have been more than appreciated.

Contents

INTRODUCTION

There are some discrepancies about being a man and being a man of God. Manhood has been stereotyped in two categories, what he can't do and what he's supposed to do. There are noticeable and recognizable differences. Men are supposed to be in control. They are supposed to be fearless and courageous. Men are expected to take care of everything and fix the problems. We keep hearing terms and phrases like, "Man up!" " Be a man!" "Act like a man!" Usually we hear questions like, "Are you a man or a mouse?" or "What kind of a man are you?" There are attacks on manhood and men's self-worth, because of how the world views and defines the role of a man.

A man of God and of grace fears God. He loves God, honors God, worships God and Praises God. A man of grace obeys God. A man of God who is growing in grace doesn't know everything but takes comfort in knowing someone who does. When he fears God, he is feared by the enemy. When he loves God, he loves everyone. When he honors, worships and praises God, it's with everything in Him. And when he obeys God, he obeys Him completely without reservation. One of the biggest comments and myths is that "Men are not supposed to cry." I'm here to bust all these myths.

This book is full of short stories, essays, poems, wisdom, prayers and life lessons I learned, gained, and gleaned from my journey in this process. You see, I don't profess to have arrived, but I am continually in a state of becoming. My story reveals the uncovering and growth of love, faith, and courage to name a few of the nuggets covered here. I am hoping that from my stories, poems, wisdom and life lessons you gain something valuable you can use in your own life, personal, professional, or spiritual development. I want to show you what growing into a man of grace looks like. I hope you are ready to take this journey with me.

CHAPTER 1

THE BEGINNING SEEDS OF LOVE & FAITH

LOVE

Love never fails. But where there are prophecies, they will cease; where there are tongues, they will be stilled; where there is knowledge, it will pass away. For we know in part and we prophesy in part, but when completeness comes, what is in part disappears. When I was a child, I talked like a child, I thought like a child, I reasoned like a child. When I became a man, I put the ways of childhood behind me. For now we see only a reflection as in a mirror; then we shall see face to face. Now I know in part; then I shall know fully, even as I am fully known
(1 Cor 13).

In the Summer of 1969, I was born, Daryl Dalton James. I was the one and only son of Donald and Coralita James and the middle child between my beautiful sisters, Donalda (Donna) and Patricia James. As the middle child of two beautiful sisters, my role allowed me to fill the void as the older brother and the younger brother. Mostly because I was the only brother.

Because of my sisters, my mom taught me how to love and respect women. My mother raised me to be a gentleman. She raised me to love and fear God. She raised me to be considerate and kind. She taught me how to love and how to give. She has imparted wisdom and understanding that has made me the man I am today.

I lived a pretty good life, resided in a house with a narrow front yard and a backyard full of wild trees, plants and flowers. My parents were from St. Johns, Antigua. They came to America and created a life for themselves while building a family.

LOVE

Do you know what love is? Love seems to be the most misunderstood and misinterpreted word in the English language. Perhaps this is where the confusion comes into play. We actually don't know what love is. If I were to try to define it, it would be the act of selflessness and sacrifice.

Like most kids, when I was younger, in elementary school, I just wanted to fit in. I went to a Catholic school. The groups to join were limited, and I had very few qualifications. Every day was a new challenge to find my place in a biased class system. You were either popular like the "cool kids," athletic like the "jocks," or smart like the "nerds." Some met all three qualities, so they were accepted anywhere. Some had various combinations, while others like me were struggling to find where they belonged. I didn't have enough friends to be popular. I wasn't athletic because I didn't like sports and believe it or not I wasn't a nerd. I abhorred reading too much to be a nerd. It's ironic, I hated reading, yet I loved words.

LOVE

Love is unselfish, uninhibited, unashamed, unconditional, unyielding, uncompromising, untied, undone, understanding, un-apologetic, un-parallel, un-toppable, unstoppable, unmoving, unraveled, unwrapped and un-warped.

English was my favorite subject and I took delight in writing poems. I loved poems. I loved symbolism, metaphors, similes and how they worked together to create a masterpiece. I loved adjectives! I loved describing things with more than just the average word. I liked creating works that would literally jump off the page.

When rap music came out, I was enamored by it. I would participate in rap battles in school wherever, whenever, with whoever. It helped build my confidence. It gave me the sense of being untouchable. No one could handle my verbal tenacity. I was gifted with gab and vocab.

Art, another talent and gift, was my first entrance into being accepted. My teachers loved my drawings and my friends would ask me to draw them so I would. I was the one everyone called on to help them with their art projects. I used these talents and gifts to my advantage and played off my strengths.

LOVE

Love, it doesn't come with acknowledgements or recognition, but it comes with something even more priceless, freedom. The freedom to withdraw yourself from negative energies and atmospheres so that you may sow love in the areas where it's most needed and necessary, is priceless.

Girls were not interested in me like I was interested in them. I hadn't figured out how to use my poetry to win them yet. I wasn't their first choice, boyfriend, or dream date, so I lived in the "friend zone" for most of my life. I had to accept that I was different. I was shy and cautious. I was an adolescent, and still finding myself. What I did have going for me was that I was trusted. Most of the girls trusted me with their feelings and aspirations. My extreme sensitivity made me the ideal candidate to help everyone else with their relationships. I became trusted by both the boys and the girls. I was the one who helped them create and make hook ups. GOD gave me these gifts that helped me to assert myself and create a place for myself.

FAITH

Do you know what it means to step out on faith?

It means believing no matter the opposition,

No matter what you face

and no matter what you go through.

You may have to face negative forces that surround

you and cloud your inner vision.

You may have to face fake friends.

You may have to face those who act ugly behind your

back and right to your face.

There have been times even when I didn't look for

trouble, that trouble found me....

It was at those times that I wanted to run and hide

but there comes a time in every man's life when he

must face his opposition.

I was no different.

Although I grew up in catholic school my whole life, I was raised Protestant and Lutheran. My father's church was Protestant and my mother's church was Lutheran. My mother kept us in church. As matter of fact, it feels I've been in church my whole life. I went to church every Sunday alternating between my mothers' and fathers' church. My saving grace was that they both believed in God and the blessed Trinity.

FAITH

My faith has brought me through sorrow, pain, hurt, harm, sickness, obstacles, near death experiences, trials, judgements, hatred, jealousy, finances, despair, divorce, loneliness and transitions, health issues, homelessness, exhaustion, doubt, temptation, lies and deception.

Me and my sisters were taught from the very beginning to believe in God so strong faith was not just a priority but an asset. My mother, father, sister's and myself would read passages from the bible and pray together every Saturday morning around our parents' bed. Afterwards, on Saturday's there would be some adventures that we would do as a family. Whether it was going to the movies, going to Rye Playland, which was an amusement park, or just enjoying some time by the water in City Island. Those were times I relished. As I grew older, those times became fewer and farther between. Like most couples during that time period of the 80's, divorce became the norm, so eventually my parents split up.

FAITH

Faith is to trust, believe, and know that God will make a way! He always has and he always will. If it wasn't for my faith in God, I don't know where I would be or who I would be. It's because of my faith in God, that I no longer worry. My thoughts have changed.

I knew who GOD was, I just didn't know what He wanted me to do. When I graduated I ended up transferring to an all boys, catholic high school. I asked the Lord, "Lord, What manner of cruelty is this...? What, NO GIRLS?" Somehow I found my way. I used all my gifts and talents there as well. God graciously gives great gifts of goodness! It's time to let my light shine and allow my gift to be heard in both spoken and written word!

CHAPTER 2

GROWING IN FAITH & SELF DISCOVERY

Faith is such an extraordinary thing! Faith in God can move mountains. It can make the unattainable attainable, the unexplainable explainable. And the explanation is God...What else could it be? He is the Author and Finisher of our faith.

Rap music was running rampant. It was taking over the airwaves. I took my verbal skills from rap into high school. High school is where I made a name for myself. Then one day I got my big break. I heard from some friends that there was a block party. It was taking place just around the corner from my house on Belmont Avenue. It was being hosted by the legendary, Grandmaster Flash.

I was super excited and nervous. When I arrived, I saw that Grandmaster Flash was on the turn tables playing a lot of break beats. He opened it up and gave the invitation for anyone who wanted, to get on the microphone. Suddenly people were pointing towards me. They were pushing and encouraging me to get on the mic. Some of the acts that had gone on before me didn't seem that great. One of my friends commented that they weren't as adept as they thought they were. Finally, I stepped up. It was now or never. Grandmaster dropped the beat. I placed my hand around the microphone and held it tight. I said,

"I'm the son of a "D"
The brother of a "D"
My name is I Code
Name D-Ski
Since way back I still don't regret
My attachment to the 4th letter of the alphabet
Which is "D"
My Desire, My own Denotation
I Devastate then Debase
Then show Disintegration
Of my opponents
in a moment I will Demonstrate

13

The Devious tactics that Dispatch
the high score I rate in the ring,
I'm the king or the great contender
You will surrender to D
the Defender I do remarkable justice never do
dramatize
Simply a 'razzle-Dazzle" to release my disguise
You see my Hip-Hop hazards have hoovered hypnosis
Yet simultaneously sending out my Doc's Diagnosis
...."

I rocked the mic and the crowd went wild. This was the day that the neighborhood took special notice of my lyrical skills. Grandmaster Flash gave me a high five and told me, "That was fly!" You see people knew I could rap but they didn't know I could rap like that. I caught the eyes of a brother known to the neighborhood as Spud. He eventually introduced himself to me.

Spud thought that I had what it took to join his crew, K.O.B which stood for the Kool Out Boys. Spud was like the, "The Fonz" from the Tv show, "Happy

Days," and I was like, "Richie." Spud was known almost everywhere and well respected. He was also a graffiti artist whose artwork was amazing.

We entered rap shows and contests and won. We came close to many record deals, but none panned out. It started out as a four man group. Eventually it became just me and Spud. Spud became like a big brother to me. He always looked out for me. I believe this was because he could see I was naive to certain things. After all I grew up living a sheltered life.

In school, I engaged in many lyrical battles in the lunchroom and crushed them all. I became really cool with a fellow classmate named Dorian, rap name, 'Disco D." He was one of the few people who could match my wordplay. Our rhymes were completely phenomenal. It was the perfect combination. We recorded some songs together.

Disco and I had our issues and things didn't work out their either. I went on to become a part of a neighborhood crew called, "Rock On Productions."

The group consisted of the leader, producer and manager, Kevin aka K-Love or K-Rock. There was also Brian aka B-Fresh, Bryan aka Krazy B, me, D-SKI and the DJ, Cutmaster aka Cut La'Rock. We recorded many songs. The record industry didn't like our blend of artists. This put a wedge between us and we started doing solo projects. We were all talented in our own right. Each tried to make a mark in the music industry Eventually we realized that it wasn't going to be as easy as we thought. Although I was a wordsmith, in each group I always maintained that I was a Christian first and foremost. I was considered the "Pastor" of the group. Since I did not and would not curse or use profanity of any kind, in many ways I kept the group wholesome.

FAITH

Faith without works is dead. To step out on faith means to believe with expectancy not knowing when to expect it! It means to trust God because he is able! It means to put it in his hands and not worry! It means to be encouraged by his word and nourished by him. It means if you can talk the talk, you can definitely walk the walk simply because you believe.

In Cardinal Hayes Highschool, I decided to try a few new things. I tried to get involved with sports. I tried running track. I became good at relays in the armory and 440's. Reality hit me when I ran cross country. Cross country was out of the question. That's when I learned I didn't have endurance.

Next, I tried football. I actually made the team as a tight end. The training was intense. The calisthenics were gruesome. It felt like it was never-ending. I was a tight end who rode the bench for most of the season. I can't remember playing in any game. Apparently, I did it for a year. As stated, I wasn't into sports. They just weren't my thing.

Next, I tried band. Everyone wanted the drums. I was in the marching band where I played the coronet. I was assigned a brass instrument that I didn't want. Out of all my new ventures playing that instrument was the only thing that stuck. I marched, played it at every football game, every parade including the Macy's Thanksgiving Day parade, and every year for four years. Ask me if I play that thing now and I would have to say, no.

FAITH

So, let me ask you some questions, how strong is your faith? Has it been sustaining you? Has it kept you vigilant against the enemy? Has it kept you aware of the spiritual warfare we're in? Have you recognized your blessings? Have you understood your purpose?

Attending an All-Boys High School wasn't all bad. We still connected to the "All Girl High Schools" for events and social gatherings, especially plays. However, the stigma of my social awkwardness was not over. As a freshman in Cardinal Hayes High School, it merely worsened. I didn't seem to be anyone's cup of tea or catch of the day. Even my younger sister got upset about how many girls were dissing me. Then one day, it happened. I went out for a walk around my block. I was headed back and getting ready to come up the sidewalk of my street. That's when I saw this beautiful young lady standing on her stoop. I doubled back. I saw her smiling, but she kept looking away. She seemed shy. I wanted to approach her, but my track record wasn't the best. I chickened out and turned to walk home. Just when I went to turn and walk home her younger sister, yelled out, "She wants to know your name!" I stopped dead in my tracks, turned around, "My name is Daryl, Daryl James," I yelled back.

LOVE

Love has a way of finding us at our weakest and giving us strength to see the possibilities. We will be hurt, suffer rejections and setbacks but love can and will sustain us and replenish us where we need replenishing.

PUPPY LOVE

Her name was Diane. There was an instant attraction. We ended up liking each other so much that we quickly became boyfriend and girlfriend. All of a sudden, I exuded a certain kind of confidence that no one could take away. Now I had someone who not only liked me, but she loved me. We became inseparable. We did everything together. I was new to this relationship stuff. As a result, I mimicked one of my friends. My friend Spud and his girlfriend dressed alike with matching outfits, so Diane and I did the same. I brought us matching sweatshirts that read, "Daryl hearts Diane." I messed up. Both shirts read the same thing. But one should've said "Diane hearts Daryl." We got over it quickly. I made it known how I felt about her. We enjoyed every minute we spent together. She was my senior prom date and our colors were black and pink. I rented a limo, chauffeur and the whole 9 yards. She was also there for when I barely graduated from high school. I still had to go to Summer school. She made it all bearable. For once, I wasn't someone's last choice. She wrote a letter to my mom, stating how she felt for me. My mom still has that letter to this day.

LOVE

Love is patient and kind. It does not brag or boast. It is sincere. The love of God is pure without restrictions, but the love of mankind is perverted, twisted with an agenda. "Love me or else," is the concept we live with today. If you love me you will do this. If you don't love me, keep it moving, and don't waste my time.

If the Ten Commandments could be summed up in two sentences it would be.... Love God. Love others. Think about it, if you love others would you steal, covet or kill? If you love God these thoughts would not even take place in your heart.

The love we all need is the love that God gives constantly and continuously, UNCONDITIONAL. There are no conditions or restrictions because His love is pure and free whether you choose Him or not.

He has never stopped loving us. While we have stopped loving Him whenever it is convenient for us. We have become hypocrites. God is love, love Him unconditionally as He does us and truly feel His presence.

21

My upbringing became riddled with strife. I had a strong bond with my mother and suffered a disconnect with my father. After all those years trying to get his attention, I always wondered why my father never really took any interest in me. My father, Donald, was the disciplinarian while my mother, Coralita, was the coddler. Everything that I couldn't get from my father, I got a surplus from my mother.

LOVE.

"For GOD so loved the world that HE gave HIS only begotten SON. GOD is always giving, and HE wants to bless us beyond belief. Love with all your heart, mind and soul and feel the freedom. Experience the freedom and live the freedom like never before. GOD is LOVE and LOVE is freedom.

I was considered the "Goodie 2 shoes" because of my upbringing. I was very comfortable in my identity and my faith, so I had to find someone else who shared my perspective.

CHAPTER 3

GROWING TAKES COURAGE

After I barely graduated from high school. My last year consisted of completing summer school. Immediately following graduation, I enrolled in New York City Technical College in Brooklyn. I decided to study Architectural Technology. Ever since I graduated from elementary school I wanted to go to Art and Design school. For some reason, I thought utilizing my artistic ability would result in a lucrative career. That was a bad idea and sadly untrue. Unfortunately, I did four years in an all boy high school without an art program. I entered the program very underdeveloped in my skills verses my classmates.

While in college, I got hired at the Internal Revenue Service (IRS). The job was literally 5 minutes away from my school. It was around this time that I met a musician named Jerry. Jerry played keyboards and bass guitar. He shared my faith and perspective. We started working on songs and doing shows together. Our performances garnered some attention from a magazine editor named Kat. Kat thought that we had what it took to make it. She pushed our recordings to record executives. She got us in the door of some very important meetings. It was such an exciting time.

When we finally sat in the record company office across from these big wig executives, I was told that I needed to be more like Ice Cube. "Gangsta Rap is trending," said the Executive. He said, I was too clean. I didn't take their feedback well. I refused to compromise my integrity. This would be the first of several rejections from others like him. I was getting frustrated because of the roadblocks I kept running into. Then one day my manager, at the time, got a call to work on a song with Rockwell.

Rockwell was a group who did the hit song, "Somebody's Watching Me." We arrived at the studio. I looked up at the sign on the wall. "Laughing Dog Productions," impressively stood with its letters spelled out. It was like I had reached a new level. The caliber of artists and musicians that came through that place was mind blowing. They invited me to rap on a song called "Rock it, Rockwell." I rapped my lyrics on it, but the song was never released. I was told, I need to modernize my music. I entertained the idea before agreeing. They took my track and updated it. I recorded it but they didn't do anything with that either.

Finally, they asked me to do a Christmas rap. It was similar to using the sample from "Backdoor Santa," but they made their own version of it. They asked me to do a "Ghetto depiction" of Christmas. I did but they weren't completely happy with the results. They decided to still work with it.

I was trying hard to figure out how I could meet the producers in the middle to give what they wanted, be myself and still provide quality work. However, no matter what I implemented, it wasn't fully received. We tried one last track. They said I wouldn't have to write anything but merely recite some lyrics on a song called, "Crosstown Traffic." Again, nothing happened with the song. By this time, it became evident that I wasn't what they were looking for.

BE ALL YOU CAN BE

I was 18 years old, fresh out of high school. My music career was at a standstill and didn't seem to be going anywhere. I enrolled in college but was having a hard time at home and failing in my major. My professor advised me to withdraw. He said, I was holding up the class. I was devastated. The great thing was I had a job. Working my IRS job was ok, but one day I decided I needed a change. With the various failures in my rearview, I thought I needed to make something of myself. What did I do? I decided that I would "Be All That I Can Be," in the Army Reserve.

To fulfill the Army's requirements, I took a leave from my job at the IRS. I was under the impression that since it was a government job it was safe. I did have one concern; it was for my feet. I long since had problems with my arches. I expressed my concerns to my doctor. He said I should ask my recruiter. "We have plenty of soldiers in the army with flat feet, you'll be fine," said the recruiter. That was the end of the conversation. I was later picked up at home by the same recruiter. My mom and sister's saw me off. I said my goodbyes to them and was on my way. On the trip headed there I was full of nerves.

COURAGE

I have been down but not out. I have been hurt but not scarred. I have been lost but not wayward. I have been stranded but not desperate. I show courage not conceit. I give respect not malice. I am my father's child and he is in me.

The next thing I knew, I was in a room full of recruits reciting an oath. In February of 1988, I took the oath to support and defend the constitution of the United States in that room with all the other prospective soldiers. Then I was on a plane to Fort Bliss, Texas. We were flown to Fort Bliss, Texas for basic training and a rude awakening. Once we got off the plane, we were quickly given an abrupt introduction. After we arrived to one of the scariest introductions imaginable by our Drill Sergeant, Sergeant Gilyard, our heads were shaved. For those of us who had facial hair, the haircuts involved, removing our mustaches and beards Next we endured a rigorous cavity search. We were given a full body cavity search to make sure we didn't have any hidden contraband.

The experience reminded me of an old movie I'd seen before. It was like the scene out of the 1989 movie, "An Innocent Man," starring Tom Selleck. In that movie, Tom's character was arrested for a crime he didn't commit. He was then taken through the process of becoming an inmate. We belonged to the U.S. Army now. It was pretty clear to all of us there, that life would never be the same again. I was in a whole different world now where I planned on studying to be a medical specialist.

Next, we received our GI's (Government Issued) gear. We were stripped of all of our civilian clothing. The government gear consisted of camouflage fatigues, underwear, socks, t-shirts and boots. Once I got into the camouflaged gear, put on those long green socks, followed by combat boots, pain shot through my feet. My feet hurt so much I thought I was wearing high heels. "Oh, my Word, I could barely walk in them," I thought. I tried to take one step and literally fell flat on my face. I was immediately transferred to a medic.

The medic doctor said, you have severe pes planus which is another way of saying "flat feet." He suggested they do surgery to have arches surgically implanted in my feet. refused. If GOD didn't make me that way, then it wasn't meant to happen. Meanwhile, they tried jungle boots which is made of a softer material around the foot, but the arch pain was still there. I was then put on what was called a soft shoe profile. This pretty much meant I was able to wear the New Balances I came there with. In addition, I had to walk on crutches. The doctors asked how in the world did I get recruited with my feet. I told them that it was a concern that they took lightly.

My drill sergeant saw I was lagging behind my platoon because I couldn't keep up trying to do hikes at 3am in full gear on crutches. I was sent to Central Quarters awaiting my papers to be sent home. I was there so long that I was able to see my company prepare for their graduation from Basic Training. In March of 1988, literally a month later, I, Daryl Dalton James was expeditiously separated from the United States Army Reserve with an honorable medical discharge. I finally returned home. Unfortunately, I wasn't there long enough to claim any benefits. To top it all off, I lost my IRS job.

COURAGE

The words discourage and encourage both have the words courage in them. To be discouraged means removing your courage to try. Being encouraged means strengthening your courage to succeed. Be encouraged not discouraged because encouragement makes things change and change makes things happen.

I became depressed about my future. After a considerable amount of time, I bounced back. I started doing temp work. I worked for various companies under minimum wage without benefits. I even worked for a foster care agency called Richard Allen Center on Life where I was a file clerk. Again, I was building friendships and met some very interesting people. Budget cuts caused my departure from that job.

Leaving the service was a hard pill to swallow but I still consider myself a former soldier. I still wear my hat with pride. My duffle bag goes everywhere I go. There were a few positives that I took away from the experience. One plus was that I went in 225lbs. and came out a solid 180. However, my feet never recovered. Later I was hired at Harlem Hospital Center making more money than before. Soon I got an apartment. I moved out from living with my girlfriend at that time. Nothing went as I planned but it definitely was a learning experience.

CHAPTER 4

POLICE BRUTALITY, FAITH & FREEDOM

Time marched on. I met a young, chocolate-toned, beautiful sister named Ronda. People called her Purple because she loved the color purple. Purple was eccentric and unique. We met at a house party where we danced all night into the wee hours of the morning. We went on dates. We hung out a lot and really enjoyed spending time together. Eventually this grew into a closer connection. We decided to become a couple. Her children seemed to adore me. I loved them too. Everything seemed to be going in the right direction. I was pleased.

I had just turned 21. I was still "fresh, wet behind the ears," as the old folks would say. A young man just starting out on his journey. The vivid memory is stained in my mind like fresh paint on the wall.

It was a few days before Valentine's Day. Purple's birthday was also right around the corner. I decided to take a trip to Canal street to get her something nice. I was shopping for my new girlfriend. It seemed like the best place to find a nice gift. I rode the train and enjoyed the sound of the wheels on the tracks. I found it relaxing. Once off the train I headed up the stairs from the platform and onto the crowded street. The choices of stores were endless, as I strolled, and plodded along, taking in the sights. I traveled in and out of stores, perusing, and examining one item after another. I searched until I found the perfect set of gifts, a beautiful 14 karat gold chain with a locket and a teddy bear for her. After I found her gifts, and the corresponding card, I ducked into a small café shop that sold sandwiches, coffee and tea. I ordered a hot tea, pastrami on rye, toasted. "Hold the tomatoes, I told the man behind the counter. As I ate, I thought more on love…

Why are we so afraid to tell someone we love them? You should be aware that you could miss that opportunity to say " I love you" to someone before it is too late. Life is short, never hesitate to sow love, then show love. Tell someone you love them today. I love all my brothers and sisters! I love you!!!! " You should love your neighbor as you love yourself"...........Set yourself free in God's great love........I did, and so can you. Let's not be afraid to love!

After I ate, I headed back out into the night. I was walking along towards the train. I was headed for the station to return home. I was anticipating the reaction that my girlfriend would have from the gifts. I crossed the street at the light. I descended the stairs back to the train. It was no sooner than I stepped my foot on the platform that I was surrounded. Police officers seemed to appear from every direction. I stood frozen like a deer caught in the headlights. One of the officers quickly charged towards me and within minutes was on top of me.

FAITH

What does your faith say about you? Is it, immense faith where you never ever worry or is it just enough to get you through? Truth is, it should never be a contest that measures whose faith is greater, but it should be the incentive to rely completely on GOD. The world doesn't see what spiritual eyes see. The world is of flesh and displays fleshly things.

"Freeze!" "Hands up!" he commanded. He positioned himself in front of me, his arms out in front of him, his feet in a fighting stance of twelve and nine o'clock while pointing his gun in my face. I quickly shot my hands up in the air, eyes wide as I dropped my gift on the ground and the contents of what was left of my tea spilled down my side. It was within seconds that the other five officers were there surrounding me with guns drawn.

FAITH

I was reminded by my sister in Christ, Jean Rawls, that "Faith is already in you but for many it lies dormant because of nonuse. Faith is like a muscle, it needs to be exercised to built up, so you can see what GOD truly has for you and not be consumed by doubt, fear or self-loathing." I decree and declare that I want everything that the devil stole from me and I want everything that GOD has for me.

"Get down on the ground!" His partner in an instant shot past him, jamming his gun that was drawn back into his holster before grabbing my arm and twisting it behind me. I had already begun to lower myself to the ground, as he slammed me the rest of the way. I laid there with my face to the concrete, tasting the dirty platform in my mouth. My mind raced trying to understand what was happening.

"Don't move, or I'll shoot!" he shouted now with his knee in my back. He pulled my other arm behind me to handcuff me. I couldn't stop shaking as the policemen handcuffed me.

Do you know the reason why God said, Without faith, it's impossible to please GOD?? Because without faith, it's impossible to know GOD. Without faith, it's impossible to have a relationship with GOD. Without faith, it's impossible to connect with GOD. Think of it this way, how can you pray to someone you don't believe in? How can you recognize the purpose on your life when you can't acknowledge the one who gave it to you? Faith goes beyond the visible, the understandable, the reasonable and takes you straight to the unfamiliar, unfathomable, incredible and impossible. I encourage everyone reading this to really let go of the comfortable and security and embrace the unimaginable and unthinkable because that's what GOD wants to do for us. All you need to do to begin this wonderful journey of wonders and favor is have faith.

"God have mercy" I exclaimed loudly. The officers who had now relaxed and put their guns back in their holsters seemed to all turn simultaneously in my direction. My life flashed before me because I didn't know my fate. I thought my life was over, I was shaking and feeling frail. My nerves were on edge because I still didn't have a clue what this was all about. I already knew several guys doing time upstate for crimes they didn't commit.

FAITH

Have faith my brothers and sisters and watch how God works. Have faith in HIM, choose faith and watch what happens.

The other officer lifted me to my feet and threw me against the wall. They transported me to a nearby makeshift jail. They booked and fingerprinted me. Beads of sweat poured down my face and I continued to shiver and shake uncontrollably even behind bars.

"You're a big guy. You play football or something?" said one of the officers trying to console me. "Yeah, sure," I said nervously, voice trembling. "I played some in high school, but it wasn't really nothing.

FREEDOM

Our rights afford us certain freedoms. Freedoms and rights, they may be said and thought to be equal but they do have differences. The freedoms we have are constantly being used haphazardly. What exactly is freedom? When you talk about freedom, justice and the American way, what does that mean?

What did I do?" I said as my mind began to gain some clarity. I took this open invitation to now try to appeal to him.

"There was a robbery in the area, and you fit the description."

"I fit the description. What description?"
"Black male, yellow shirt, black shorts."
Looking down at my clothing, a lime green shirt and blue shorts, I then looked back up at him.

"It will all be over soon so don't worry." He dropped his head down and he went back to filing his paperwork.

39

"I didn't do this. I didn't do anything wrong. Officer what is happening? Why am I just sitting here?"

"We are waiting for the victim to come down here and positively ID you. Just sit tight." They all looked away and no one else talked to me after that.

FREEDOM

We live in the land of the free but how free are we when certain freedoms are not acknowledged in certain areas? It seems we are living in the land of the free that is losing its' freedom. Now freedom comes with many restrictions. How is that free? Our freedoms are being taken away from us and slowly rendering us helpless and powerless. There doesn't even seem to be a democracy anymore. To many of us are being discredited, disavowed, disallowed and disrespected. How much are we truly valued when our rights are constantly challenged or disregarded?

I sat inside that jail for what seemed like an eternity.

"We have your perp Ms. Kim," I could overhear one of them on the phone.

An hour went by before the short, thin, frail looking Asian woman came down. They pointed her in my direction.

"We found him trying to escape and board this train, a few blocks from your shop Ms. Kim," said the officer with slick black wet looking hair. She came closer. She squinted her eyes further trying to get a good look at me. She looked me in my face and then looked me from head to toe.

"No, that's not him," She said immediately.

FREEDOM

The root word of freedom is free, right? So what's free anymore? Anything free now comes with a price and so does freedom. If freedom is the result of being released from bondage, what bondage have we been released from? Sin is the freedom to do wrong thinking that there are no consequence.. We play the blame game often to free ourselves from blame but we're not really free. We're merely prolonging the inevitable. When you take ownership of the blame, you free yourself from the pain of continuous lies and suffering.

"Were Sorry," the police apologized. The Italian looking cop opened the cell and took off my handcuffs. "Here you go," he said returning my things, a damaged Valentine card, sorry looking bear and smashed gift box. They released me. My stomach felt queezy and my knees felt weak.

I couldn't help but think of so many Black men that I knew were doing time because of mistaken identity. It turns out that the suspect was a Latino male wearing a yellow top, black shorts and white sneakers. He was of a thin build while I was a black male, husky build, wearing a lime green shirt, blue shorts and black sneakers. How does anyone make that mistake?

I am living proof that faith works! He did not bring me this far to leave me (Genesis 22: 1-8).

Although relieved about the outcome, my heart was still in a sling. I shook all the way home but thanked

God for His compassion. I know the devil's busy and he works in every fashion but God intervened like when an attorney objects in a courtroom. I see now how God has always been with me no matter the season, predicament or the reason. God has been with me no matter the dilemma or problem. It doesn't matter at all, He will never forsake you, all you have to do is call.

FREEDOM

In America you have the right to choose. Some died for their rights since their choices were freedom or death. What if your freedom is found in eternal life? I got good news, Salvation is free. That's what Jesus is offering constantly, repeatedly, without fail. Your choice. Who the Son sets free is free indeed. God loves us so much that He gave us the freedom to choose Him. The world can't give you what God has already given you. Remember we must be in the world not of it. All power was given to Jesus when He rose from the dead. No weapon formed against us will prosper and the devil has no power or authority.

Jesus died so we would be free from all sin. However since we were given freedom you can choose. Who or what will you choose?

CHAPTER 5

FINDING PURPOSE REQUIRES LOVE, COURAGE, AND FAITH

*Courage is standing firm in the face of adversity.
Being courageous is having unwavering faith when
all odds are against you. Only faith in GOD brings
courage and boldness.*

I was hired in the Building Services Department as a housekeeper at the Harlem Hospital Center. The job came courtesy of Donna, an old friend of my sister's, who helped me get my foot in the door. Finally, it was a job with steady pay and medical benefits. My first since the IRS. My job, dangerous at times, was relatively simple, clean up infectious waste. I swept, mopped, removed trash and medical waste. Later, I learned how to strip, wax and buff floors. Eventually, I developed a persistent cough that agitated my lungs and made it difficult to breathe. I was later diagnosed with tuberculosis. My doctor cited the infectious waste exposure.

No one ever said that faith is easy because it isn't. No one ever said that there's nothing to worry about when you have faith because there's a lot. Faith simply roots your position in GOD's plan. You've accepted HIS guidance, protection and direction into your life. You know you're not perfect, but you serve a perfect GOD. Your faith in HIM says you trust HIM. Your faith in HIM says you honor HIM. Your faith in Him says you'll serve HIM. Your faith in HIM says you love HIM. I know it's a struggle, but the rewards are more than worthwhile, they're priceless. They cannot be matched by any worldly possessions. Nothing worldly can compare to GOD'S Word! HIS word is incomparable and distinct. Some do their best to dispute it, but you can't dispute the undisputed. You can't conquer the unconquerable. You can't rewrite what was never yours to write. It is written means it was done so why are we trying to do it over? Faith as a mustard seed is not just referring to its size. A mustard seed is strong and pungent. The taste does not waver. It's long lasting, a lot like our faith should be.

When the president of the Local Union Chapter 420, Zonzie, heard about what happened, she immediately had me removed from housekeeping. I was transferred to the mailroom. I went from wearing a uniform to regular clothes. It was a welcomed change. The mailroom was adjacent to where the infectious waste was delivered, so not much changed.

Harlem had several buildings. The mailroom was responsible for all of their mail delivery. The various buildings were always buzzing with people and activity. As a housekeeper and later a mailman, I met and engaged with many people. I met Daz while working in the mailroom. Daz was an astute, clean shaven and well-dressed brother. Daz had heard about my rapping talent. He had mentioned introducing me to some of his connections. He believed he could do more to help my career.

Harlem had an event for Secretary's Day, a talent show. I decided to participate. Daz was there and heard me rap. It wasn't until he saw me performing at the Secretary's' Day Talent Show, that he said, he knew I was worth the investment.

After that talent show, I became much sought after. At the event, I was approached by a representative of the Montel Williams Show. She asked me to be a guest. In my mind it was a no brainer. So, I quickly replied, "Yes." The representative said she loved what I was wearing. I wore a hunter green two piece suit with black patent leather shoes for the show. Under the suit, I wore a white shirt with a kente cloth tie, vest and matching handkerchief. She asked if I could wear the same outfit to the show.

I was so excited that I told everyone I knew. I requested the day off from my boss. I made sure I had my winning outfit on for the show. The producers gave me a time to report to the studio. I arrived bright and early. I shook Mr. Williams hand and greeted the other male guest. Unbeknownst to me, the show was called "School teacher makeover." I was selected to be a prospect for one of the teachers. Come to find out, the other men who were there were prospects as well.

As Montel welcomed me to the stage, there was applause and then I was seated. Montel asked me to tell his audience a little about myself. I was told, I appeared sweet and succinct on T.V. Montel however was informed that I could rap. He asked me to give my audience a taste. I did. This is what I recited.

LOVE
"It's like the beauty of the rainbow that falls down as rain
The definition of love cannot be explanation.
A devotion between a couple through trials and struggles
Surrounded by nature and life simply juggles
Truths and lies and lies and truths
Answers to these philosophies bare no proof
But I assure that my lure will secure you even more,
Why? 'Cause my love is pure."

The audience erupted with applause. I was thinking that by being on national television that surely someone of power and influence would see me and like what they saw and heard. I returned home and some people recognized me. Unfortunately, it wasn't the exposure that I needed. I just couldn't make any headway.

I met another young brother named Jeffery. Jeffery was extremely talented himself. He said, he loved my performances and wanted to work with me on my music. He was one half of a duo called Twice, made up of him and his twin brother Darrell. He and his twin brothers performed together and sang songs they created. It was a nice change of events. Dealing with brothers who wrote and produced their own original material was inspiring Something wasn't gelling there either. I felt like I was weighing them down. After a few shows and recordings, I decided to move on.

PURPOSE

Harlem Hospital was downsizing. This created a window of opportunity. The hospital gave employees the option to be bought out. It was for a fraction of their salaries. I jumped on it. I couldn't see myself growing or going anywhere in that position. I decided to instead, embark on a new adventure working for United Parcel Service (UPS) in Manhattan. It was right off of the Westside Highway. I was one of many hired as a drivers' helper. The position was seasonal. I was hired to work from October until the New Year.

I was all set to work through the holidays. I was hoping and praying, the job would be a Segway, leading to an offer for a position as a permanent employee. I was excited to get started. My manager handed me my uniform, a pullover jacket, hat and pants. He informed me that the employees would have to provide any other clothing needed to stay warm during the winter months. The winter was brutal and the snowfall heavy that year. The work was intense

51

when it came to the deliveries especially attempting to trudge through the snow.

I made it through the holiday season and was asked to be a permanent employee. The permanent positions came with full-time benefits even if you worked part time. I along with several other workers who were called back were assigned as permanent driver helpers. While the work was strenuous the hours remained low unless you were requested by the driver to stay overtime. After 3 years working part time, I felt unfulfilled. I needed more. So, to combat this, I decided to take on a side gig. I applied and was hired at Tiffany's as a night Porter. Juggling both left my sleep diminished. Sadly, I didn't keep that job.

I have been told that if you love what you do then you've found meaning but is that your purpose? It is so easy to enter uncharted waters with the goal to tread through it. What if you're purpose is much simpler than that?

"Your gifts will make room for you"(Prov.18:16). This verse has no substance or power if you don't know what your gifts are. I've learned that there's a difference between your talents and your gifts. Your gifts are not your talents and your talents are not your gifts. Our gifts are for a purpose. God has designed each and every one of us with a purpose, for a purpose. We all have a purpose, meaning everyone was created on purpose for a purpose. Every life has meaning and purpose but we all also need direction.

Wouldn't it be nice to know what your purpose is? If you knew your purpose then you wouldn't have to aimlessly keep exerting your energy on things that you weren't purposed for. Could you imagine the impact it would have in our lives? The purpose that is meant for us comes with incredible benefits. Could you fathom the unlimited blessings to follow? Can you envision what levels of success we would be able to attain? What plateaus we could reach or favor we could gain if we just knew the purpose He has for our lives? The benefits of our gifts are called favor and increase which are unlimited. Don't you want that?

What would you do if you found out that the purpose you were pursuing was not yours to pursue? What would you do if the reason you weren't successful in the field you chose was because it wasn't your field to choose? Is it possible to simply not know what you want or not know what you were made for?

Is it me or does it feel like there's something in you suppressing your positivity? It seems there is some battle that is creating negative thoughts and energy? Do these thoughts seem to be keeping you from succeeding and living your best life? Are there too many things to deter, dissuade and prevent you from living in your full potential?

Every setback or delay that keeps us from pursuing GOD turns us away from living in our purpose. Anything stopping you from reaching your full potential, robbing you of time to make your dreams real, keeping negative images and discouraging remarks in your mind, heart and spirit, is nothing but the plan of the enemy. The enemy wants you to be distracted. He wants you to lose focus, momentum and desire to aspire. It's a plot to keep you broken, hurt, in self-doubt, and anguish.

Living in the flesh will get you fleshly things. While, living in the spirit will get you spiritual things. You can't live in flesh and receive spiritual things. You can't be of the spirit and receive fleshly things. The problem is that we misunderstand the two and miss our deliverance.

Think about this, most people who go into college have no clue of what to pursue. They take electives to find out what drives them, sparks them and motivates them. They search for their passion and convictions. Everyone is on this search to discover who they are and what are their gifts. I share in this never-ending quest to find who I am and what am I supposed to be doing. We all neglect the fact that God has the answers.

I've seen many people, including myself, take courses and receive certificates for careers that do not suit them. Or worse I've seen them enter professions that didn't bring them satisfaction or gratification. Sometimes, we get caught up in our own heads about our choices or follow someone else's dream. Chasing someone else's dream doesn't make it yours. It's ok if you don't know what you want. It's not ok to follow someone else's dream and make it yours.

The easiest thing in the world is to concentrate on what you can't do. Learning what you aren't called to do frees you in the discovery of what you can do and are called to. Some of us are heavily entrenched in areas where we should not be because we're not aware of where we should be or who we are. If you're in this state of bewilderment and confusion, you are in desperate need to turn to the one who made you with a purpose.

PURPOSE

I believe if you don't see the potential in the gifts that God has given you, no one else will. Trust and believe that you are destined for greatness. Just because you're not where you want to be doesn't

mean you won't get there. The key is not to become
or stay complacent. That slump that you're in won't
last and that pressure on your back won't remain.
Things may be moving slowly at this point. You may
not see it right now. Success doesn't look like it's
around the corner BUT GOD'S word cannot return
void. Void meaning empty and without credibility. It
will set out to accomplish all that He said. That
sounds like a promise.

The truth is we've been asking the wrong question. It's not, "What has God done for us?", but instead, "What hasn't GOD done for us?" In a message entitled, "Working the System," Pastor D clarified what is the system. He refers to the System of God highlighted in Matthew. He illustrated that God's System has not changed. The Word has always worked. It worked then (in ancient times) and it's just as effective now. Even from the passages where God used Moses, His system is still the same. The first step was and still is to seek the kingdom of God in heaven. Seeking first the Kingdom means; seeking God in everything we do. Seeking first the Kingdom doesn't mean just in prayer and supplications although that is the starting place. Seeking GOD first gives Him the opportunity to take you where you never thought you'd be. Instead of making rash decisions in finances and life changes, we seek Him for the answer. When going through difficult choices or feeling pressured to come up with an answer, we seek Him first for a solution. We shouldn't be leaning on our own understanding when He is just a prayer away. The Lord will be there no matter the case or situation. We've all tried to do things our way for way too long. God's system has not failed the believer whose faith is strong in Him.

Seek ye first the Kingdom of God and its righteousness and all these things shall be added unto you (Matt 6:33).

Pastor D further emphasized on the discrepancy between the actions found in this scripture of "To give" and "to add." If something is given to you then it can always be taken away but when something is added to you it becomes a part of you. Essentially it is yours.

You shouldn't be putting God into your life but instead putting your life into God. God wants you to have all things, not just some things. When you adamantly seek His face in all you do, you will know what His true purpose is for your life. When you do seek Him, His kingdom will come into your life. So, when you first seek His kingdom, (God's kingdom in heaven), all these things will be added unto you.

I am always being challenged at Impact Church. The leader said, that if we weren't hearing from GOD, that it was a heart problem. He contended that GOD speaks to our hearts. The Pastor went on to say that if it's not GOD'S voice we're hearing, it may very well be our own. Some things we may see posted or hear from someone else may be good, but it may not be GOD.

I can admit that I am so eager to hear HIM speak to me that I may believe HIS voice is my voice. How do we know the difference? HIS Word doesn't return void, mine does. HIS Word is precious and truthful. His Word needs to be in our hearts so we can connect what we hear with His Word on a spiritual level.

Ask yourself, what's keeping you from moving forward? What's stopping you from living your purpose driven life? What's separating you from HIS love? What's causing you to give up, throw in the towel and yield before the start of the race? This race can only be won moving forward. You can't look backwards because it turns you completely around. You can't look to your left or right because it takes you off the path. If you're not following GOD, you leave yourself open and vulnerable to other things or people to replace HIM.

You will never find satisfaction without finding your true purpose. Take your time. Explore. Learn more about yourself and what drives you. We don't have to keep searching for things that leave us empty. God wants us to be fulfilled. Lean on your Father in heaven. God has a way of tying things together to bring you clarity. He's awesome like that. He knows what each, and every one of us was designed to do. He knows what our purpose is so we don't have to keep guessing. What God has for you, is for you, and you alone. No purpose is the same. God knew you before you knew yourself. Your purpose was ordained before you existed. Whatever you do, make sure you do it for the glory of God. Whatever you started, don't stop. Wherever you are, don't stop. GOD will make a way for you and bring many things to your understanding.

God knows us, inside and out. He knows the purpose for each of us.....just ask Him. HE wants you to live in your true purpose. HE wants you to have all that you desire (when those desires come from Him). HE wants you to use your gifts and talents. We are His created masterpieces. We are masterpieces of Almighty God. Make the light within you shine so bright that there is no mistake about where it came from. We are all called to be ambassadors of Christ. We are to be servants to Him and His people.

We have value. We have a purpose. We have meaning. We are because HE is. If you really want GOD to move on your situation, you must connect to HIM through the Spirit. He's in you. Take that leap of faith and walk boldly in the Spirit and watch GOD move. Will you trust HIM??

GOD is omniscient because HE knows ALL THINGS! HIS comprehension is beyond ours. HE knew us before we knew who we were. Some of us are still trying to find ourselves and figure out our plans. Truth is we're already FOUND. It's already FIGURED out. FAITH is allowing GOD to control our outcome without our interference. We have a habit of getting in our own way and blocking our own blessings. Remember, my purpose is not your purpose and your purpose is not mine. The plan that GOD has for you is unlike any other. Just because the endgame is the same, (to bring souls to Christ), doesn't mean our gifts must match. GOD gives us the grace to grow and mercy to change so that we can embrace the call HE has for each and every one of us.

Jesus came for a purpose and completed His mission. It's time to take note and follow His lead. Procrastination builds regrets making your to-do-list impossible to get done. Don't let setbacks, delays, distractions, interruptions, inconveniences hold you back from finishing strong. Remain steadfast. All things are possible to him that believes. All things are possible to those who stay focused and do what needs to be done. Your focus should always be on the one who created you on purpose for HIS purpose. It will give you peace of mind and lift your spirit. BUT GOD will withhold no good thing from those who walk uprightly. All things are and will be used for our good. I needed to say that for myself and I hope someone else is also encouraged to maintain. GOD gets the glory because HE is GOD

Being Christ-like is knowing God's purpose is bigger and better than any circumstance, situation and dilemma that any man, woman or child may encounter.

CHAPTER 6

RACISM & PROTESTING IN THE LAND OF THE FREE, HOME OF THE BRAVE

Me, my wife (before she passed) and a few other people were in a conversation about the injustices taking place in our society as well as the response. The response to the injustices are enough to set us off and keep us flabbergasted. I can't, for the life of me, figure out why our peaceful protests have caused so much tension in our country. I am still in awe by the insensitivity and the disregard for our people in this country. It's appalling. Here are some of the conclusions I've come to....

Racism is alive, well, and running rampantly in this country. The truth will come out eventually. While America has great elements, we can't deny that the system is broken. The SYSTEM WAS DESIGNED FOR some of us TO FAIL. With that being said, the intentions have been to keep the classes separated. The system is designed to help the rich get richer and the poor get poorer. Think about it, people are being deported at a rapid rate. Many of our people (Blacks), are being shot and murdered in cold blood. Many may be tired of hearing about black men being shot and killed by police officers, but many of us are tired of living this nightmare over and over. We are constantly harassed and made examples. We can't even protest peacefully without our lives being in peril.

It seems the only way we're really heard is through protest. I am truly hurting because it seems no matter what we do, we're wrong. We protested in the 60's, we got hosed down. We protested in the Olympics by standing up with a fist in the air and we're criticized for that. Now it's kneeling, arm in arm, and that's another issue. What exactly are we supposed to do?

FREEDOM

Being righteous is doing your very best to live right but being free is knowing the unlimited potential that God has given you to receive His blessings abundantly. The freedom in the Spirit is exactly what it is, freedom.

My mind is and has been blown by those who are angry about protesting peacefully. I cannot comprehend the logic for their anger. Nowhere is it written that anyone has to stand for the National Anthem. There's nothing in the constitution that says we're supposed to stand up for the flag, so why are we being reprimanded for kneeling? Kneeling is the most honorable position imaginable. It displays submission, honor, respect and reverence. Now there are talks about making it a law to stand for the National Anthem. Why? Is it because one man decided to take a stand against injustice, police brutality and the murdering of innocent Black people? Is it because he sacrificed his career and income for this cause? Is it because this peaceful protest is unifying various races, creeds, colors and beliefs who believe enough is enough?

FREEDOM

So, I get it. I get it about living in the land of the free and being patriotic about this great country we live in. I get how we endured so much to be free in this wonderful country. I even get what freedom fighters, abolitionists, civil rights activists, pacifists and organizations of peace were assembled for and what they were fighting for. What I don't get is why haven't we fought for, hungered for, desired, craved and yearned with the same passion the sweet freedom that our Lord Jesus Christ offers freely???? C'mon and be set free!

My pastor, Pastor D even commented that despite the things happening, we can still thank God that we're not where we were or use to be. We have come a mighty long way. I agree. However, I can't help but wonder why must we experience so many setbacks to move forward? God put us all on this planet to love one another, work alongside and respect each other. I don't wish any harm to any race but it's time for change. My GOD is merciful and ever faithful, so all my trust goes in Him.

On the other side of Racism, we see the contrast of America's makeup. America is made up of a beautiful, diverse, multicultural, multinational and multifaceted people, who live together, work together and love this country. People have come from all over to find opportunities and brand new lives. Many have found whatever means to make their dreams a reality.

Freedom to love. Freedom to care and share. Freedom to honor and praise. Freedom to live in peace. Freedom to acknowledge who is the one who gave you freedom in the first place. Freedom is priceless.

In times of turmoil and catastrophes, this country has always come together to show how strong and resilient we truly are. There is a kindred spirit that we have seen bring us through triumphs and tragedies. In the devastation of 9/11, there were no limited, separated or divided thoughts, feelings or beliefs being expressed. It appeared everyone wanted to help each other. There were no discrepancies about who was going into those towers. Everyone went in and it didn't matter the color. Black, White, Brown and every nationality worked together tirelessly to find survivors. They went in to save who they could and lay to rest who they couldn't. People risked their lives to save others. Strangers became friends and gratitude became a significant gesture that was often expressed.

Today, as brave individuals risk their lives, endure hurricanes, tornadoes and even pandemics to save others, we should remember that they don't have to do it, they want to do it. There seems to be a love for God's creation that surpasses human comprehension. It's something that happens spiritually when people step out of their comfort zones for their fellow American. We were made to love and care for one another.

"Greater love has no one than this, that someone lay down his life for his friends," (John 15:13).

Our first responders risk their lives daily without hesitation and without concern for their own safety. They are seen in every tragedy, natural disaster or just for someone in need. I salute the men and women who risk their lives to save others without prejudice or bias. If you live in this country, in my opinion you deserve to be here. If you fought to get in this country, you have a right to be here too. If not then what does that statue even stand for anymore? I thought liberty was freedom. What does the Statue of Liberty really stand for?

"Give me your tired, your poor,
Your huddled masses yearning to breathe free,
The wretched refuse of your teeming shore.
Send these, the homeless, tempest-tossed to me,
I lift my lamp beside the golden door!"

Noam Chomsky, renowned researcher of linguistics, said that people have the natural instinct to help one another. However, the system has been rigged, brainwashing us to believe that we can make it on our own without anyone's help. The system has been designed to separate us. When we subscribe to statements such as, "Every man for himself," "I gotta get mine before you get yours," "Do you," "Look out for yourself," and these kind of beliefs, we become a divided people who can't work together or get anything accomplished. Even Jesus taught us that, "A nation divided against itself cannot stand." In unity there's STRENGTH. You weren't meant to do it all by yourself. In unity there's FREEDOM.

There's peace in freedom. There's joy in freedom. There's strength in freedom. There's endurance in freedom. There's love in freedom and this freedom cannot be taken away. Let's get free people. Let's take the blame for what we did and get free. Freedom is priceless and ironically, it's free. Take advantage.

Knowing that you're not alone frees you from fear, hopelessness and doubt. In unity there's LOVE. Caring for one another and sharing with one another removes hatred. Helping each other embodies the love that Christ exhibited on the cross. In unity, we can look forward together, progress together and make a difference. United, we stand. Divided, we fall. We are all Americans. We have heart. We have strength, we have courage and we can have love for our fellow man. God bless each and every one of you and God bless America.

Father, I ask that you remove hatred, malice, indifference and hurt from my heart. Help me to be strong with people who aren't who they claim to be and love them anyway. Give them open hearts to receive Your love where they can empathize. God increase our faith and help our unbelief. Grant us the strength to fight and push forward. Let nothing separate us from Your love. We need You more now than ever. There are dark forces in high places that denounce You and treat You with disrespect. They do not know that You're omnipotent. They do not know that You're omniscient. They do not know that You're omnipresent. They don't know You. But we the believers, know You. We stand on Your word. We walk by faith and not by sight. We love You, honor You, magnify You and glorify You. You are worthy to be praised. Lord hear our cries, our pleas and our prayers, In Jesus's name we pray. AMEN.

CHAPTER 7

RIGHTS, LIBERTY & THE PURSUIT OF HAPPINESS

We live in a world where no one believes that they're doing anything wrong. No one wants to be responsible or held accountable. The liberties that we fought for are often taken for granted and abused. We are all living on borrowed time. Our freedoms like our rights are in danger of being taken away from us daily and permanently.

God used the army and being a former government employee to teach me quite a few things. Mostly they both taught me about Freedom and Rights.

Politicians pass laws. Soldiers fight for our protection. Attorneys fight for our civil rights. There are doctors and nurses who fight for the right to save lives. Why?? All because of human rights. We all have Rights.

Everyone has rights even thieves, criminals, and murderers. There are the Bill of rights which gives us and them the right to due process. Anyone arrested has the right to remain silent. They have the right to an attorney. They have the right to be judged by a jury of their peers. They have the right to a fair trial. Anyone has the right to come to this country legally and make a new life for themselves. You have a right to live, raise a family, grow old, and be buried here. You may have a birthright to be here. You may have to work hard to earn your legal right to stay here. You have a right to be treated fairly and to live free. You have the right to not be judged by the color of your skin but by the content of your character. You have a right to live wherever you want and can afford. You have the right to access assistance to government programs and resources where available. You have the right to pretty much do whatever you want.

It seems we've gotten spoiled with all these rights. Maybe we have taken for granted that we could exercise our rights when and how we chose. For instance, criminals may have the right to free counsel, the right to be silent and say nothing when arrested but if convicted they can lose their freedom. For the 2.3 million guilty and at times wrongly accused in this country some of their rights have been lost. However, it appears that even the everyday citizens are slowly but surely, starting to see our rights removed. How long before we don't have any? The truth is, it will be a different situation if your rights are taken away permanently.

Many died so we could have the opportunities we have today. They have given us the chance to make a difference and a change. While it may seem that our say doesn't matter, our opinion doesn't matter, and our vote doesn't count, we still remain indebted to those who paved the way for us to have these rights. The question becomes how do we repay that awesome debt? What if our ancestors didn't believe we were worth the sacrifice? What if they had never faced being beaten, spat upon, treated with disrespect, hatred and malice?

Let me introduce you to a new Bill of Rights. You have a right to live holy. Anything you say can be used against you or the devil in the court of The Most High. You have the right to counsel. If you cannot afford one, Jesus is a Lawyer in the courtroom. Also, the Holy Spirit has been provided for you. Its up to you to just ask Him into your life. Do you understand these rights?

The truth is, even greater than what our ancestors did, no debt was greater than the one Jesus paid. Jesus died because you matter. Jesus died so you could have eternal rights to the Kingdom. Jesus died so you didn't lose your entitlement to the kingdom. What if Jesus didn't believe that we were worth the sacrifice? What if Jesus thought differently about asking HIS Father in heaven to forgive us for all we did to HIM?

We are under the greatest attacks from principalities, and forces in high places. Every day our nation is facing bigotry, misogyny, prejudices, biases, and favoritism with no regard for the well-being of GOD'S people. Maybe you don't care about voting but if you no longer had that right, would you care then? Vote like your life depends on it because in my opinion often it does.

CHAPTER 8

FRIENDSHIP & ENCOURAGEMENT

Unfortunately, today's world has a warped and twisted definition of friendship. Some friends are not good friends. Some are bad influences and if you continue the relationship they will lead you down a dark path. If you associate yourself with troublemakers, not only will trouble follow you but even if you haven't done what they've done, you could still be in a lot of trouble because that's called "guilty by association". Some are negative and want to bring you down to their level of being miserable hence why misery loves company. Some are jealous and envious of what you have and will go through extreme means and measures to take it from you. We often criticize others and make them feel less than.

Our church often teaches us how valuable friendships are. I remember one Sunday our Pastor focused the message on the question, "What kind of friends do you have?" He encouraged us all to get out of relational poverty. A lot of us make friends because of the surroundings we frequent such as work, school, or the gym.

He mentioned three types of friends from his message "Good Together," from the "Together" series. There was Samuel: A friend that makes you better (1 Samuel 16:12-13, NIV; Proverbs 27:17 NLT). Jonathan: A friend who helps you find spiritual strength (1 Samuel 23:15-16, NIV). And finally, Nathan: A friend who tells you the truth. (2 Samuel 12:7, NIV; Proverbs 27: 5-6, NCV).

How many of us have these kind of friends? If you look at all of these characteristics, they define what actually makes a good friend. Someone who makes you better, helps you find spiritual strength and tells you the truth. These three characteristics represent real friends.

There are different kinds of friendships that play significant roles in our lives. There are the "seasonal" friends who are there for a season. Many of these encounters while short, definitely still make an impact. There are, "The Sometimes," friends who are only there some of the time. There are, "Long Distance," friends whose friendship never seem to cease. Long distance friends are the type that once you get back together, you don't skip a beat but pick up right where you left off.

Then there are, "The True Blue," friendship. That's the kind of friend who never leaves you hanging or abandoned. They are the reliable, dependable people in our lives. What's significant about a "True blue" friend is their desire to see you to succeed in every facet of your life. Within these types of friendships, there's no room for envy or jealousy. The true blues encourage you to aspire towards greatness. If you fall, they are there. If you make a mistake, they forgive. If you run into any difficulty, they want to help you figure out what's the best course of action to remedy your problem or situation. They are supportive. They are honorable and respectable. Most of all, they make you accountable and responsible by telling you the truth. A "True Blue" friend will tell you both the good and bad. They desire for you to grow. With a "True Blue" when it comes right down to the nitty gritty, you can count on them. I believe that's what we want and should try to be, "A True Blue Friend."

A friend is a person that no matter what you're going through is there for you. A friend is a person who gives it to you straight without sugarcoating it. A friend is a person that defends you and supports you but is never disrespectful on purpose. A true blue friend is a real friend. Real friends want to see you succeed and want you to have the best that life has to offer. Real friends want to see you prosper. Real friends go out of their way to help you get what you need. Real friends are trustworthy and show concern for your wellbeing. They are compassionate towards your feelings. They are in your lives to make it better not bitter. Real friends are not just assets, they are essential for growth and community. Real friends do real things in real life.

Sometimes you have to wonder if you have real friends or fake ones. You know what I'm talking about, "Fairweather friends." The ones who are only there when things are good. These are the same friends you can't find them when situations take a turn for the worse. The ones who smile in your face and talk about you behind your back. You have to wonder if that's how GOD feels.

Some only call on HIM when things are bad. The scripture (Psalm 34) reads, "I will bless the Lord at all times." There's no room for sometimes. Some of us talk about HIM as if we think HE can't hear us. We may be perpetrating a fraud ourselves. We want good friends and a great GOD but what if we are the fake ones?

Some of us are around enablers, the ones who keep telling us what they think we want to hear. They appease us instead of telling us the truth. Some of us are around envious people, who want what we have so they pretend to be our friends to be around us. Some of us have "self-centered, attention seeking friends."

82

They are the ones that think only about themselves, forgetting about you, and leaving you out whenever it's convenient for them. Some so called friends want to tell you everything about yourself but never address what's wrong in their own lives.

Lady Terri, really delved into what creates that unbreakable bond in friendships. She highlighted a friendship that truly stands the test of time. Some of us have friendships that are dead weight. Misery loves company. These friends aren't doing anything, so they don't want you to do anything either. When dealing with these kinds of friends we must look at what the scriptures says. How can two walk together, unless they be agreed? "Show me your friends and I'll show you your future." You might be just one friend away from a better future. If friends are supposed to be supportive and caring, ask yourself this question, "Are my friends dragging me down or lifting me up?"

To be unevenly yoked does not just apply to marriages, it can also be applied to friends. It represents friends who don't work well together. There could be two people who are combative with each other. What you will see is one pulling one way and the other one pulling the other way while neither get and go anywhere. However, marriages should be two friends embarking on a life journey together in sync and one accord.

Proverbs 13:20 says, *"Walk with the wise and become wise, for a companion of fools suffers harm."* If you want to be wise, surround yourself with wise friends but foolish company breeds foolishness. If you want to be wealthy surround yourself with wealthy friends. Being broke around other broke people will keep you broke. If you want to be better, surround yourself with better friends. If you're complacent and do not desire growth then misery will keep you with other miserable people.

In another series entitled, "Reaching Friends", our pastor preached several messages to help us fully comprehend what a friend is, what a friend does and how to be one. As he highlighted, a friend is someone who is regarded highly but doesn't do it for the accolades. We need good friends, real friends. Friends who are in your corner, supportive, caring, loving, selfless, truthful and spiritual. A true friend treats you the way they want to be treated. What greater love is there than one who lays his life down for a friend? What a friend we have in Jesus! Jesus said that there is a friend who sticks closer than a brother. What have we done to earn such love, support and encouragement? What have we done to earn such loyalty, honor and generosity? Christ thought of us enough to say that we deserve all of that and more.

Widen your perimeter and engage in long-lasting, non-toxic, fun-filled, growing, developing and mature friendships (Acts 9:26-28, NIV). Our goal should be simple, be a good friend to others. In return, they can be a good friend to us. The ultimate goal is pleasing God so that He calls us friend. Since the passage reads, "Do unto others as you would like them to do unto you," how are you doing unto others? Are you being a real friend? Ask yourself, are you a good friend to others or do you take advantage of other's friendship towards you? How much do you value your friendships? Do you respect them enough to allow your friends to grow even if it means without you? Are you truly there for them when they need you? Do you actually know how to be a friend? In other words, do you know how to care for others other than just yourself? When your intentions are pure of heart, you will reap the benefits of that friendship. The question is, Are you a good friend?

ENCOURAGEMENT

I want to give you some words of encouragement. Sometimes we can lose focus by focusing on our independence. We often focus on what we don't need. As a matter of fact, we can be so caught up that we become oblivious to the things that we do need. There is nothing wrong with receiving affirmation on the path chosen in order to be effective. There's nothing in the world like being encouraged when feeling discouraged.

A very enlightening conversation with my brother, Ryan from Impact, revealed how we can't expect to get out of our current situation without determination in us. The motivation has to be within us. To piggyback off Pastor D, if it's only on or in your mind, you'll probably succumb to negativity and negative self-talk. On the other hand, if it's in your heart, you'll do whatever it takes to achieve it. It's so easy to lose hope and live in despair. While courage makes you defy doubts and face fears.

I learned another valuable lesson from my beloved. Most people never think about how the one who encourages needs encouragement too. Think of all the wonderful people who encourage and inspire you to aspire to new heights. There may be those in your life who push you to reach goals plus keep you grounded. They usually are self-less and their efforts are tireless. They wear smiles that are genuine. They have hearts that are open towards others. They carry themselves as true servants of the Lord. However, do you think that they never experience weakness or setbacks? As a matter of fact, it's just the opposite. Praise GOD for all of those beautiful brothers and sisters who encourage others. They are the ones who put all their fellow brothers and sisters needs ahead of their own. None of their good deeds have gone unnoticed. Trust me, GOD sees everything.

As Christians, our faith takes serious beatings by unbelievers and naysayers. A wise and wonderful woman, Tina Adam said, that we're only under attack because we are valuable and have value. Think about it, a thief doesn't rob an empty house.

Our faith needs to be in the one who walked on water, healed the sick, turn water into wine, made a blind man see and a dead man walk. We need to look to the one who was wounded for our transgressions, bruised for our iniquities, and died for our sins. He was buried and rose from the dead meaning he conquered death so we may have eternal life. Jesus Christ is who we choose to follow and spread His word. We're talking about a King who did more in His 33 years on earth than we could ever do in several lifetimes. He is the greatest encouragement known to man because what He did was while He was in human flesh. In addition, before He left, He sent someone to keep us encouraged, the Holy Spirit.

God's hand in the form of the Holy Spirit in our lives makes the difference. When Christ is at work in our lives we will see the needed changes for the better. What is the point of living life without God? Without Christ in our lives, it will result in an aimless waywardness. It becomes utter and complete foolish and fruitlessness. Aren't you looking forward to hearing, "Well done my good and faithful servant?" I know I am, and this is the only encouragement I need. I feel a freeing to leave the world of empty excuses and unfulfilled promises making success my destination.

Get away from discouraging people and keep the people who encourage you close. My brother Lorenzo always told me to stay encouraged and even though I thought I knew what he meant, but I was only partially correct. To stay encouraged means it's ongoing and it never stops. The enemy is busy, and he wants you to concede and fail. Stay encouraged.

CHAPTER 9

MARRIAGE, FAMILY, CHILDREN & RELATIONSHIPS

Her name was Sharon and she was incredibly beautiful. We met online. She said she was going through something herself. Her then husband, had a serious problem with cheating. She explained that she had given him more than enough chances to change and fight for their marriage. She said that after nine years, she was done. I had my own situation I had come out of with my first wife. As I pondered this new woman in my life I couldn't help but think about what it meant to be together.

When you hear the word "together" do you actually know what that means? Doing things together seems obsolete since everyone believes they should do things on their own without anyone's help or assistance. When I think about that word, I think about unison, union, joined, connected, combined, unity and in unity there's strength. Too many people get in relationships and simply take over and dominate. They have ideas of their own on what a relationship is and how it should be. It's very one-sided without any consideration of the other person's feelings, hopes or dreams of an ideal relationship.

Sharon and I decided to finally meet in person one day. We planned to see each other for the first time, face to face at the 33rd Street train station where the Path train came in from Newark. Newark, New Jersey was where she was born and raised.

As I waited for her, I looked for the colors she said she would be wearing. I searched and searched but didn't see her. She snuck up behind me and covered my eyes. She said she was a little nervous meeting a stranger for the first time, so she lied about what she wore.

When I turned around, I couldn't stop smiling. After my eyes viewed her from head to toe, I was in love.

She was a thick, lovely, honey coated almond sister. She had the most enticing chestnut brown eyes, cute button nose and luscious lips. Under the most adorable hat, she had a low haircut which beautifully framed her face. She wore baggy jeans, a pullover fleece hoodie, and gortex boots. It didn't matter how baggy her clothes were, she was absolutely breath taking. She walked with such grace and femininity.

I saw her full figure and was mesmerized. I didn't want to make her feel uncomfortable, so I moved slowly, attempting to just enjoy her company. We were in Manhattan Mall and decided to get something to eat. Sharon ordered a filet-O fish meal with a medium Sprite soda. I ordered my favorite, a double quarter pounder burger with cheese meal with a Dr. Pepper. As I was standing in line waiting to order, Sharon felt the urge to press up against my back holding my hands. I had chills going through my body. I love affection. When I retrieved our orders, we sat in the dining area below to eat and talk. I expressed how much I enjoyed what happened and would like more of that. When it was time to leave I leaned in for a kiss. We kissed so tenderly. It was amazing.

Neither one of us wanted to leave the other. She came home with me without any regrets. From that day forward we were inseparable. She made many trips to the Bronx to spend time with me. I travelled on occasion all the way to Newark just to have lunch with her. This was the happiest I had been in years. She echoed the same sentiments. Things soon became even more serious with us as she introduced me to her mother, Peggy. Her mother expressed that she was glad to finally meet the man who swept her daughter off of her feet by way of the internet. Then she introduced me to her sister who suffers from mental health issues along with another sister who she said was her foster sister. Her sister who had mental health issues had a son who Sharon affectionately called "Booga." Sharon and her ex use to take care of Booga but Booga and Sharon had moved in with her mother after her ex was served the divorce papers.

Sharon would travel to the Bronx even on Sunday. Sometimes making more than one trip. She invited me to her church, The Tabernacle Church in South Plainfield New Jersey. I went there twice and enjoyed both services. The first Sunday I attended I heard the senior pastor preach. The next Sunday it was his mother. It was powerful but way too far to travel every Sunday. However, I promised Sharon that if I ever had to move to New Jersey, I would join her church.

It's amazing what God will do at the right moment. He will work everything together for our good. That means he uses both the good, bad and ugly. It just so happened that after about 2 years, I was served with an eviction notice. When I appeared in front of the judge, he said, "Technically, we can't hold you responsible for any past rent because your name is not on the lease." He said, "If you can move out in the next 2 months, this whole case goes away." I took it as a sign and told Sharon to start looking for an apartment for both of us. I needed to go, and she was cramped living back at home with her mother. She was sleeping on a bunk bed with her foster sister while her nephew slept on the couch in the living room.

Sometimes, it's so simple that we miss it. We miss it so much that it's a shame. The reason why we miss it is because it has never changed but you think it has. It has never been acknowledged but you think it has. It's in every discussion, conflict, disagreement but never resolved. When you can admit that something is wrong or doesn't seem to be working, you're halfway there to discovering what's needed to make the necessary changes.

We found an apartment on South Orange Avenue in Newark. We pleaded with the landlord to take a chance on us. I think he saw that we were young and just starting out, so he did. The budget was $800. Somehow God made it work. We were able to afford $200 more in rent yet still pay for our utilities and other expenses.

I kept my promise and joined The Tabernacle Church. I have to admit that I enjoyed every minute of it.

Sharon worked as a librarian assistant for an agency called ProLibra. Her job kept her pretty busy until her health became a problem. There were days that I would get a call because she passed out and had to be admitted to a hospital. I continued working different jobs, none of which were stable. I was too busy worrying about Sharon's health.

We discussed the idea of marriage. I was a little apprehensive. My track record wasn't exactly the greatest. I asked her, "Would you really marry a man who's been married twice before and has children?" "Yes," she answered, without skipping a beat.

We truly loved each other. I had never experienced a love like this before. So, I asked Sharon to marry me. We officially were engaged. We proceeded to get a marriage license and started marriage counselling with Pastor D and Lady T at Impact Church. We informed them that we were indeed living together. Immediately, they instructed us that we needed to practice abstinent. Pastor D told us that if the urges became too much to bear we could call him. He said, he had trust in us that we would do what was required. He said, "Remember this is between you and GOD."

Unions are strong because there is power in agreement.
Two cannot walk together unless they agree.
There is an undeniable strength that is visible when two walk in one accord.
When two become one mind, they become one entity and what God has joined, no man can separate.

The sessions were incredible, informative and life changing. After 8 consecutive months we grew impatient. We wondered if it was possible for Pastor D to marry us in his office. We asked him and he repeatedly said no. He stated, he didn't think we were ready.

The divine order is God first, family second and everybody else third.
Sometimes the order is not correct therefore it presents issues with confusion.

God must be first in all we do and say for without
Him, there would be no us.
Love is not enough to sustain a healthy relationship
with your partner, spouse or significant other but
God is.
God is Love.
God is Creator.
God is Father.

It was a Sunday morning, August 23rd, 2009 to be exact. Sharon and I woke up, ate breakfast, and dressed in our coordinating colors as usual. On this day it was sunny yellow tops, indigo jeans and white sneakers. We left our home to meet the church van set to pick us up and take us to church. As we entered the sanctuary, the presence of GOD filled the place making worship intense and memorable. We went to our seats and listened to the sermon. The spirit was so intense that most of the congregants came up to the altar including Sharon and I. While I was still at the altar, the Pastor asked,

"Brother Daryl, are you ready to get married?"

"Yes Pastor," I said.

Sharon had already turned to leave and was headed back to her seat. She was redirected by Brother Donnie the armorbearer to return. When she returned, Pastor D asked her the same question.

"Sister Sharon, are you ready to get married?"
"Yes Pastor!" She said.

"Hold on y'all, we about to have a wedding!" The congregation had already begun to leave and head home when the announcement stopped them all in their tracks. Pastor D, asked another Pastor to retrieve his bible from his desk. One of the church sisters ran to get Sharon's mom.

"Your daughter is about to get married!" She screamed.

It was totally unexpected. Pastor D had been resistant for the past 8 months. He was not exactly in agreement because he believed that we needed more time.

"On this Sunday," he said. He had heard from the Holy Spirit and his wife, Lady T confirmed it. He proceeded. As soon as he read the words, "Dearly beloved," tears came down on both of our faces.

We were in complete amazement that this was really finally happening. Sharon and I were both on our knees as we were pronounced man and wife. I tried to keep my composure, but I had never been happier. There wasn't a dry eye in the sanctuary.

On August 23rd, 2009, after 8 almost 9 months of marriage counseling under Pastor D and Lady T, a man and a woman were joined together in holy matrimony by the power of the Holy Spirit. By the time we finally got married, our license had expired.

We ended up getting remarried in our pastor's office the following Sunday. On August 30th, 2009, our pastor joined us again into the sacrament of holy matrimony. It was finally official that Mr. and Mrs. James were hitched. We had endured so much. Unbeknownst to us, there was much more to endure. I made a vow to this woman before God that I would love, protect and be faithful to her. What God joined let no man separate! We were so in awe that a year flew by. It is true that time flies when you're having fun.

"She's is the queen of my heart," played, and was the song I sang to her by El DeBarge. My heart was overwhelmed by this incredible gift that God gave me. I've had my ups and downs but never enjoyed the journey as much as I did with Sharon. She was the blessing that God bestowed upon me. She used to say, "I talked too much." I did. I blamed her because she gave my heart so much to say.

People often ask me all the time, "What makes a good marriage?" I believe what they are really asking is, "Is love (or loving each other) enough?" Well, love is a beautiful, necessary and essential principle. However, in my opinion you won't get very far if you don't at least like each other. I haven't had as many years as a lot of my fellow married couples under my belt, but I believe from my experience I could tell you a thing or two about love.

One thing that is getting lost, is the, "art of dating." Dating seems to have become obsolete and outdated. Why doesn't anyone want to get to know each other anymore? Why aren't people interested in taking time to invest in a friendship? Why are so many going straight into a relationship? I will admit that Sharon and I leaped into our union after our first meeting. However, our story doesn't account for the time we spent getting to know each other online and by phone.

As I look out on the dating landscape, I can't help but wonder what happened to romance and taking things slow? Turn on just about any radio station and even the songs are talking about jumping right into the bed. It seems to be more about sex camouflaged as love. What happened to the substance, beauty, mystery, anything?

Most relationships end because neither person knew the other. They find out things later. Many times, these unexpected revelations leave the other party unwilling to continue in the relationship. Can you blame them for not wanting to deal with something after the fact? Sharon and I told each other everything. We started out being open and honest. We laid our cards out on the table and let the other decide if they wanted to continue in the relationship.

When it comes to relationships, the root word is "relate." Often people skip getting to know one another and jump headfirst into waters they are not prepared to delve in. If you cannot relate to each other, how can you be in a relationship? If you don't talk and get to know one another, how can you grow closer together? If you don't share things together like, experiences, moments, encounters or quality time together, how will you know if you even like each other? Most relationships end because they never really knew each other.

In these situations of the hidden reveals, it would have helped, and saved each other time had they gotten to know one another first. Seriously, how well do you know someone when you find out later they have a whole other family in another state? How well do you really know someone when you find out later that they have a criminal past?

God has a divine plan and His design is for us to be happy, more importantly have joy. Our Father knows best. He doesn't desire fruitless, unproductive, unsuccessful, insincere, troubling and unhealthy relationships for His children. He is good. He is just. He is loving. He doesn't want us to be with anyone who doesn't love and respect us. We shouldn't want that for ourselves. We should love ourselves as well as the one who created us more.

Many marriages fail. Many fail because they are or became two strangers. Instead of two loving individuals coming together in the presence of God, they lost their way trying to make sense out of something insensible. Evenly yoked means more than commonality, it means that the weight of the relationship is evenly distributed and carried. It means that both parties have a responsibility to strengthen each other. We strengthen each other through conversation, through connection and through conviction. Being friends first can give both people the chance to see if there is a future. If you give it enough time you may find that a friendship is for the best. God has someone for everyone, the hard part is being patient.

To "Like," someone may be underrated but it's the start that can blossom into love. If we begin with the right ingredients, our connections can blossom into healthy, loving and monogamous relationships. Our love can grow into a strong and fruitful marriage in the future.

If we want our marriages to be successful and prosperous, we must be willing to be patient, learn and grow. The wonderful years I spent with my wife were a joy and a blessing. Even with all the years of experience, I still don't claim to have mastered marriage. Everyone wants to believe that they know their spouse inside and out. Many put on a show as if everything is great. The truth is that as we grow, we change.

Marriage is a dynamic system that is ever changing as you and your partner grow and change. There will always be something new to learn. If we are growing together, we will recognize and realize the changes as they happen in each other. Often one partner in the relationship may be growing at an accelerated rate more than the other. The key is being attentive to those changes in the other as they happen.

As we relate, we must be reciprocal in our relating. In marriage, or any relationship for that matter, it would help if we understand reciprocity. Reciprocity in our relationship is understanding that relationships operate under a "give and take" system. For instance, rewards go both ways. Women have needs and so do men. Sharon and I learned that appreciation goes both ways. Women want appreciation and so do men. Acknowledgement goes both ways. Women want acknowledgement and so do men. Romance goes both ways. Romance is always portrayed as feminine and purely for the female. Men need romance too.

I also learned that it's so easy to get stuck in a routine. The redundancy of the routine can be unhealthy as well. After a while of doing the same mundane things, boredom can put you both in a rut. When couples get stuck in a rut it can be becomes difficult to get out. For example, if you both have a favorite meal you eat every night of the week, it wouldn't hurt to shake things up. You could try to venture into new cuisines and challenge your taste buds.

There is no age or time limit to change. You can be newlyweds, married for less than a year and bored. You could be bored, sitting around, praying for things to get better. You could also be married 25 years and be bored stupid. Many marriages fall apart because there is a disconnect. They could be in a situation where one or both spouses lose their connection. Some may be in a marriage yet still feel alone.

We often hear words like, "too controlling," "selfish," "stubborn" or "uncompromising". In the Word of God,

God describes the man as the priest and the woman as his helpmate. However, He does not make one more essential than the other. The Priest's job is to protect, provide and battle against anything coming against the marriage. The battle that the man has to engage in, is a daily one but he's not alone. He is not alone because his wife is in it with him. Every negative force that comes their way, they are to stand against and get through it together. They are to be a team and a reflection of the other. Because the two are instructed to become one, when you see one, you should see the other. Their love for each other and their faith in God makes them stronger together. Their faith helps them weather any storm and take on any obstacle. In a fruitful and healthy union, they each want the other to succeed. They understand that by putting the other first, they both can benefit from a fruitful, favorable and highly blessed life together. There's no fruit in being selfish, arrogant or by yourself. The fruit is sown and grown in a much more satisfying and pleasing way when couples are in one accord, doing things together.

Love in a marriage is sacrifice. It's not holding in, it's holding on. It is the understanding that our lives are intertwined in such a way that there is no separation, (impinged). "We have become one so what you feel, I feel. What hurts you, hurts me. What agonizes you, agonizes me. It's not sympathy pains but a spiritual and emotional connection that strengthens the bond. Before diving further into Marriage, we need to understand its foundation.

If you're not putting work into your marriage, your marriage won't work. By the way, Newsflash, Marriage is WORK. It is precious, essential and priceless but it's also work. This concept of the grass being greener on the other side isn't worth the trip. God is in everything and when we try to remove Him, the results are chaotic. Agreement is a powerful force because when two agree, they're heart, mind and spirit's are free. How can two walk together unless they agree? Two must be committed to each other. Two must be honest with each other. Two must love, honor and respect each other. One cannot carry the relationship for the other. A relationship divided against itself cannot stand, but a relationship, a union, a partnership, a marriage that has God as the foundation can stand against anything including time. What God has for you, is for you, and you, alone. What's outside of God's will for your life was never meant for you.

Often when two people engage by rushing into a relationship then there may also arise some trust issues. When significant other's hide information or worse yet lie to the other it may be difficult to recover the relationship. There's nothing more damaging to a relationship than the loss of trust. There is pain that results from lack of trustworthiness. I think it's a fair assessment that the offender is not cognizant of the hurt and betrayal the other person is feeling. When you can't trust the person you entrusted your heart, what's left? Promises to change and do better become nothing more than chatter when the act is repetitive. Seeking to throw blame around doesn't deal with the issue. Making excuses doesn't fix the problem, it actually exacerbates it. How do you fix something that looks irreparable? How do you fix what has destroyed so many unions from friendships, partnerships, unions and marriages? GOD is how. There are just some things that we need GOD for that man cannot do. GOD can heal all wounds. God can heal fresh and old wounds, grudges and resentments because HE loves us. GOD heals hearts that have suffered hurt and experience depression while being under an insurmountable amount of pressure. Admitting our part in the wrongdoing that caused the mistrust is only the start to recovery and forgiveness. Healing from GOD is the remedy.

Another serious issue within some marriages is abuse. There is a serious sickness and a deep insecurity when a man abuses his authority for sexual pleasure. What kind of man feels good about taking advantage of women? The kind who thinks with a body part and seeks to have women who are in fear of his authority and status over them? It is deplorable and despicable to commit such acts.

Then there are men who step outside of their marriage, return to their spouses while leaving irrepressible memories in the minds of their victims. The sacrament of marriage obviously means nothing to them. Their vows are meaningless because they have broken trust and lives have been damaged in the process.

I pray that all of these women heal from these horrible ordeals that they endured. I pray they get everything that's due them for their pain and suffering. I also pray that these men feel the pain they have inflicted on these women, repent and turn from their evil ways. They say that time heals all wounds, but God heals all hearts.

The enemy is well aware of the potency that is present in the sacrament of marriage. The goal is to conquer by keeping us all divided and weak. The enemy attempts to insert incentives for couples to break up, go their separate ways and remain apart. It's an attack because in unity, there's strength.

God's purpose is Divine.
He is fully aware of traps and snares from which
many couples have become victims.

His (Christ) love conquers all plots of the enemy
which includes hatred, envy, infidelity leading to
division and divorce.
God is everything.

Without Him, we are nothing, plain and simple.

As a result, marriage should be supported, nurtured, and celebrated. This brings me to the topic of anniversaries. Let me explain why anniversaries in a marriage are to be celebrated. Simple, each year is a testament that the enemy failed. Each year prepares you for the next. Each year you grow stronger, wiser, more resilient to any plot or ploy of the enemy. Each year you both become a force united in agreement against the enemy and anyone he chooses to use. Each year as you watch other marriages crumble, you learn to lean on the Master first and foremost, rather than each other. Each year you value each other more because you remember where you are and who you are with. You remember how God and His infinite wisdom, knows your heart and connected you with the perfect mate. Each year represents another journey through the trials and tribulations that you triumphed over together.

I pray for those who have maintained a blessed and healthy relationship. May you remain steadfast and strong. I pray for those that have parted ways that you find room for reconciliation. Remember, who He puts together, no man can separate. My wife and I had been on both sides of the track, so by no means am I perfect. However, there is a confidence that comes when you believe God said you're perfect for each other. Your anniversary will be a constant reminder that He brought you through! It's a time to reflect and look at how God brought you together and has sustained you ever since.

Whether in friendship or marriage, no one knows or could know everything about a person. Only God knows us inside and out. The beauty of marriage is to never stop getting to know each other. Remember that there will always be more. Marriage is getting to know your special someone over and over. There is so much to explore and learn. Each day is an opportunity for this connection for as long as you both shall live. There is more to discover between the front and back cover. Read with anticipation, delight and wonder. Enjoy your mate, cover to cover while you can. I enjoyed mine until I lost her. I am a widower now and life seems strange in this stage. I never thought I'd live my life without my best friend.

I thank GOD for the gift I had in Sharon (God rest her soul) because she was my very best friend. She encouraged all my ambitions and was my biggest cheerleader. It's very rare in this life that you find someone that you really like and love simultaneously. We talked about everything and we really did enjoy being around each other. I valued her. I respected her. I encouraged her as much as I could.

She tried to do school online like me, and she started off very well, but it took a physical toll on her. We decided to concentrate more on her health. I admit that I was overwhelmed with everything that she was going through, which slowed down my goal of getting my Bachelors. However, I knew where I needed to be, and it was by her side. I knew that I was doing everything in my power for my best friend and loving wife. Even with all that went on, I managed to graduate with a certificate. She was right there celebrating. She expressed how extremely proud she was of me.

It boils down to the fact that marriage is a sacred institution. Jesus said that marriage is to be restored to the original plan which is man and wife. The Word is undeniable, remarkable and an incredible source to view man's conduct. The Word also helps us learn God's ways. We can visualize through His Words. He made his instructions crystal clear concerning what He did not accept yet man chooses to appease himself and his flesh. Just because we tolerate something doesn't mean we endorse it. We are emotional beings. We run, think and act on emotions rather than logic.

You can change your appearance, your wardrobe, your views and ways of thinking but you cannot change who you truly are. Who you truly are is who God originally created you to be. Man can change a law, but God's laws remain the same. Man has been changing laws for years. Just because laws are changed doesn't make it right. It's still a sin in God's eyes. Moses changed the law as well. Moses wrote a law allowing divorce. He may have done it to prevent hurt and harm, but divorce is still a sin. Polygamy happened in the bible but it is still a sin. Admittedly, I have sinned since Sharon wasn't my first wife. I have to be honest about that and tell you the truth.

My job as a Christian is to speak His word. Thank God for His Grace. I am not here to condemn, belittle, or debase anyone. For those of you who do not agree, I will still love you no matter what. It's your choice, but don't hate me because I'm speaking the truth. Don't shoot the messenger, as the saying goes. There's too much hatred, disagreements and disharmony. We are being pushed to pick a side. The truth is, I have better things to do than to worry about how others live their lives. I have a life of my own to live. However, I can still take time out to share truth with you in love. I trust God to be the Judge. Our God is not only just and fair, but He is also loving and true. I think of the Serenity Prayer.

"Lord grant me the serenity accept the things I can not change, the courage to change the things I can change, and the knowledge and wisdom to know the difference."

We were built by His love to love. God's word stands alone and is truly undeniable (Acts 21:4-6; Deu17:17; 2 Sam 20:13; 1 Pet 2:17; Acts 5:29; Heb 8:13; 9:27-28; John 13:35; Matt 5:44; Matt. 19:4-10).

Lord make the marriage represented for the person reading this stronger. Lord strengthen our families. Lord reduce the divorce rates, bind up and cast out divisions. Lord I give you every marriage and I pray that every marriage, be covered, protected and preserved to persevere through any storm, challenge, rough and rocky roads, obstacles, barriers and the like. I also pray that if anyone has been hurt or feels lost in their union that they turn to You, our Father in heaven for spiritual guidance and comfort to be strong and fight. I also pray that for the ones who have gone their separate ways that they be reconciled if at all possible. God you said, all things are possible with you. For those who are alone and hurting may they be healed. Lord help them find someone deserving of them. Lord bless them to not be abused or taken advantage of. Lord heal the hearts of those who are still healing. I ask this all in Jesus' name. Amen

CHILDREN

"Train up a child in the way he should go: and when he is old, he will not depart from it"(Prov 22:6).

"Brother Daryl, why don't you get the new iPhone? You should get the new iPhone, it's only $800," said one of my students.

"Only $800, huh?"

"Yeah, the other one is only $1,000."

"So, you think that is cheap?"

"Yeah," she nodded her head.

"Yes," the rest of the class agreed.

WHAT IN THE WORLD?!?! Our children have no concept of money, I thought to myself. Never mind them understanding the value. Television commercials and advertisements have given them a warped perception of real life. For some of us $800 pays bills, car notes, insurances, food, gas or could be aside for unexpected costs, rent, mortgage or a portion of it. How and when did a cell phone make the top of any list?

Remember what happened with cable? It became more than difficult to watch regular television. Cable took over the connection waves, rendering it impossible. How about the landline phone? It became a package combo bundled with cable and internet. These inventions were followed by "goodbye" landlines. God help us in a blackout and God forbid these towers go down. We live in a world where it no longer matters what you want, technology will force you to acquiesce.

Our children are obsessed and consumed by electronics. The ironic part of their expenses is the strategic plan of the digital companies that keeps us spending our money. They create one model and then constantly create more upgrades. In less than a year, or every few months they upgrade, dropping the price of the phone or electronic you currently have. The cycle continues. Soon they stop making and discontinue the brand, type or model that you're accustomed, forcing you to spend.

We spend a ridiculous amount and our kids see us, thinking it's normal. Why are we placing Jordan's on newborns, jewelry on toddlers, and designer on a child? We repeatedly buy expensive game systems because they have to have the latest. Why?!?! We are raising a generation of spoiled self-entitled ungrateful individuals.

Since when did money grow on trees? Listen, I learned a long time ago that you must work for it. As kids, we did chores. As adults, we went out and got jobs. We soon learned who F.I.C.A. was, (that dirty rotten scrondrel!). We learn to budget and live within our means. For those of us who were taught to honor and fear God, we paid our tithes. We soon found that God would give us more if He could trust us with little. We saw how the little prepared us for more. We began to do what needed to be done and watched Him add on. As far as $800 for an Iphone, we must teach our children a better way.

Let's discuss teaching our children. Admittedly, it's a fine line to walk when teaching our children. Let's ask ourselves some questions. When it comes to teaching our children do we want to change their behavior or show our power? When it comes to children, how much of a difference can be made in our wording towards our children? There are some of us right now, dealing with issues from when we were younger. Some of us still have words that were spoken to or over us that have impacted our lives. For some, it's still difficult to get pass it.

As Pastor, Nancy Salter explained, the difference and impact positive reinforcement can have on and for a child. When children are criticized and labeled with negative terminology (bad, dumb, lazy, stupid, etc.) the ill effects become nearly impossible to reverse. If and when they hear that negative talk, children are more likely to accept and believe it. They won't bother thinking they're worth it. Children tend to internalize the words spoken to them. While some internalize others will go out of their way to prove their parents wrong. How many stories have we heard of individuals who were not valued as children? These individuals report growing up feeling underappreciated and devalued even into adulthood. How should or will our children think or feel about themselves if we don't think they are (or call them) precious? What should they think, if we don't think they're (or call them) smart or blessed? If we don't think or speak highly of them then why should they? Our words are like steering wheels that can determine the path our children land on. Our first teachers are our parents. We need parents, especially fathers who will love, encourage, support, enlighten, understand, instill knowledge and moral values.

"Train up a child in the way he should go: and when he is old, he will not depart from it" (Prov 22:6). What we can take from this scripture is that Christ needs to be instilled in our early. Jesus is the way, the truth and the life. If our children don't know who they are in Christ, how will they know who they are in life? Our children face more now than we ever did. This generation is losing sense of self and faith. It's apparent that they are failing to love themselves as the beautiful people GOD created them to be.

Pastor Nay went on to say, "Just like we like to be acknowledged, praised and told how good of a job we're doing as adults, so do our children." It's important we acknowledge them for doing the best they can. We praise their best as opposed to knocking them down when they fail to reach the high expectations we often set. We can instead encourage them to reach further. Our encouragement creates a dialogue with our children that will keep them open and strong instead of stressed and anxiety filled.

Children of GOD need to know they matter. Our children need to know they have purpose. They should hear this from us, their parents. When they find that affirmation from anyone outside of us, they become vulnerable to those same individuals being in the position to tear them down. Children should always know that they are loved, appreciated and valued. The opposite can be catastrophic with serious repercussions.

Our families are and have been poisoned repeatedly by absentee, abusive parents, and the redefinition of family. The broken family system is resulting in neglected and abused children growing up abandoned, alone and bitter due to living life without love. They grow into hurt, broken bitter adults who never experienced the love and security that a healthy family unit provides. Our prisons are overrun, streets littered, bars filled, crimes and drugs rampant as the cycle continues and repeats itself when these children grow up and have children of their own.

"Finding Your Roots" with Dr. Henry Louis Gates Jr. got me thinking. The idea of that previous generations went through all they did, is not only overwhelming but also humbling. They endured so we could live the lives we live today. Most parents want more for their children than what they had. The goal is to want better for your children.

Here's my question, did we make good on their sacrifice? They obviously did what they had to do so we could be where we are now, right? Are we truly worthy of their sacrifice and everything they endured for us? If so, what are we doing to honor them?

In retrospect, even greater there's a man who came from heaven, laid down His divinity, and put on humanity. He was (and is) God in the flesh, taught, fed, healed and took on the sins of the world. He sacrificed His life for ours so that we may have eternal life. He gives us second, third, and fourth chances to get right with His Father, our Father, God by doing His will. His name is Jesus. Do you consider yourself worthy of His tremendous, selfless and loving sacrifice? What are we doing to honor Him? I know I'm not worthy but I'm so glad that He did.

IT TAKES A MAN TO FATHER CHILDREN

A father is a priest, protector and provider
who gives the Lord His proper praise to gain perfect
peace.

I remember growing up, I never dared to call my father by his first name. I knew better. I always called him daddy. My use of the title, daddy didn't mean I never knew his name. I knew his name very well, Donald Fitzroy James. I just knew better than to use it. I never understood the disrespect that many children practice with their parents today.

People have problems
that put them in predicaments from achieving
prosperity
but the power of the Potent One
presses us to pick up the pieces
and keep pushing as positive parents in position.

The difference between a father and a daddy is that a father is who you become while daddy replaces your name. Daddy's at a minimum have to maintain a physical presence in our children's lives. Too many of our young men grow up without their fathers or even a male presence in their lives. When there is an absence of the father role, many resort to finding their own role models. Many young women don't recognize what a real man, a gentleman looks like because of an absentee parent. The same young women also seek fatherhood in the least likely characters. They search to receive what they're missing. It bears repeating, a father should be the role model, holding the characteristics his daughter will later identify in a husband. Daughters need to hear and know that they're precious from both parents. Daughters shouldn't have to grow up with daddy issues because of mistreatment or absence. Sons should also know how much they are valued by both parents as well. Sons shouldn't have to seek validation from other sources leading to degradation.

Fathers, who are responsible, holding down the fort, taking care of business, educating their offspring, offering advice, giving guidance, need to keep doing so. Those who think, "it's too late, they've missed too much," need to realize that as long as you live there is a chance, possibility and hope. Some fathers are absent due to circumstances, but it's never too late. The child who is now a young man or woman is still a hurting child. Hurt doesn't go away on its own without help. Many adults still need healing from childhood issues. It may take time because healing is a process.

We serve not only an almighty God but also a loving, giving Father. Our Father gives earnestly, lovingly and freely. "For God so loved the world that He gave His only begotten son...."Don't be misled or get anything twisted, even God does not tolerate disrespect. He gives and He takes away so. He said He'll bless those who bless us and curse those who curse us. God put in His Commandments, "Honor thy father......" Remember Your heavenly Father. Respect and honor are due to Him, for all that He is, and all that He does. He deserves to be first in all you do. When God is first everything else falls into place.

Fathers, we are worthy of honor and respect as well. However, we must make sure we are doing our part and playing the role in our children's lives. God is the perfect example of how every father should be. We need to be giving, loving, forgiving but also set standards and boundaries.

Please ponder this paragraph and proceed with
precaution knowing that He is precise
and His words are precious
giving us reason to find our true purpose through His
plan.

Being a father is the toughest job you'll ever have and love. You will be relied upon and needed. You will be sought after, cared for and cared about. You have the opportunity to make a huge impact. You will command respect and have authority. You will create methods, make a difference and change outcomes. You will keep your children safe, protect them and provide for them. You will teach and raise them. You will lift them up and never let them down. You will give them opportunities to thrive and succeed. You allow them to find their way and become God fearing, responsible, respectful and productive members of society. You do your best, so they become the best. You give your all so they can give their all. You give insight so they become wise. You help make them aware and you give encouragement so that they never fall short. They will become strong and confident.

131

They will succeed because they know who their Father is in heaven as well as who their father is on earth.

A father's joy is watching his children grow into incredible, God loving, God fearing, productive, innovative and aspiring individuals. A father's greatest fear is not being around to experience his children's growth and accomplishments.

There will be plunders, plots and a plethora of poisons
to propose pathetic platitudes
to persuade you but your relationship with Him is personal.

There were two men who helped guide me into the man I've become. Both my father and my father in law impacted me greatly. Eerily or divinely, they both were born on the same date but different years.

My father, Donald F. James, went on to glory but my father in law, Willie J. Nicklow, filled the void. After my biological father left my father in law filled it in such an incredible way. I have been so grateful to him and in awe by all the things he done for me and my wife when she was here. He never hesitated to tell us both how much he loved us. I thank God for him every day and I believe my father would've liked him as much as I love him. I call him, "Daddy" or "Pops." Even though he gave me permission to call him by his first name it seems Daddy or Pops better fits.

There's a principal in the process of raising princes
and princesses to honor and respect the King.
As we prepare them for progress,
let us post His program that pertains to Proverbs
which proves our sins came at a price.

While we are on the topic of great men there are so many things to be said about another incredible man of God. I've shared many of his teaching in this book. He has impacted my life greatly. He's authentic with a deep passion for Christ. He appears to have an unquenchable thirst to keep studying the word. From what I've seen he delivers his very best sermons to his flock. He is our shepherd, our brother but most of all he's our pastor, Pastor De'Andre Salter aka Pastor D. May God continue to strengthen and lengthen his life and use him for His glory. May many others benefit from God's blessings, goodness and mercies flowing through his life.

> *There's a time to play and a time to pray*
> *and they will follow what we portray.*
> *Let their feet be planted on solid ground*
> *and their minds be patient knowing that all things*
> *are possible through Him.*

God blessed me with two beautiful, independent and highly educated sisters. I love them dearly. I have a special bond with both of them. They grew up with each other and I slightly envied them for it. Watching their bond caused me to always want a brother as well. I may not have grown up with biological brothers but God put spiritual brothers in my life. Some of these men I feel have touched, enriched, and enlightened my life. They know who they are.

One guy in particular has always had my back. He always covered me, elevated me and stood in the gap for me and my family. He encouraged me even when he was busting my chops. He said he felt my pain and insisted on helping me carry my load.

In the "Community series" at Impact Church, we learned the value of leaning on one another for support. Pastor D, taught that we're stronger together. Many of my brothers in Christ, this one in particular embodies these principles. He always tries to help people regardless of his own circumstances. It didn't matter what he was going through, he always had time for me. I can't remember a time he ever neglected me in my time of need.. I cannot hide anything from this man because he is so observant. He checks up on me and tells me he's always praying for me. To this day it's no different. He is always showing concern and has always had the ability to connect with me on a level that I never knew existed. What can I say? He's God sent. He's my brother and I couldn't imagine my life without him or his wonderful family.

I knew he cared but I never realized how much. This note of gratitude and love goes out to my big brother, Vincent Booker. We all affectionately call, Deac, short for Deacon Booker. His heart is for the Lord and His people.

Let us continue to produce, positive, patient, praying,
and willing participants that plead the blood
as we continue to protect, provide, pray for
and punish if necessary if a point needs to be
presented.

God says,... "Honor all men, love the brotherhood, fear God and honor the king." He didn't say honor some or a few men, He said honor all men. Love the brotherhood, love your brethren. Fear God. Know that everything you do holds you accountable to Him. Honor the king meaning respect the world leader, even the president.

I celebrate all fathers, grandfathers, great grandfathers, fathers-to-be, stepfathers, father figures and all men that have taken the role of a father in a child's life. Especially step- fathers. You have no idea the sacrifice of raising someone else's child as your own. These men need to be honored and acknowledged. If you fit the father role, and no one else has told you, I'm telling you now. You are all great men.

When it comes to great men let me tell you about the greatest of them all. What man is this? The man who came down from glory, left a His kingdom and throne, lived among sin without committing a sin. He taught love and peace among brother and sister. He taught us to have respect for authority, loved His father unconditionally, and served Him faithfully. He is the Wonderful Counselor and Prince of peace. His title is King, Savior, Redeemer, Healer, Protector, and Provider. He is all that and so much more. His name is Jesus Christ. He is the name above all names with all authority in heaven and on earth. If you didn't know, now you know. One who was more than man.

CONFLICT & FORGIVENESS

I thought it was important to discuss this topic in the same chapter as Marriage, Fatherhood and Children as it relates to relationships. In any of our relationships we must learn how to master conflict and practice forgiveness. Inevitably when dealing with people we will be confronted with conflict and need to learn to forgive. If we each stand on our unique positions, both believe we're right, then the only thing we have in common is agreeing that the other is wrong. Let's find the common ground of agreement, get on one accord and move forward. Confusion, monotony, repetition, and the redundancy of the argument have no place in a blessed life.

The truth is, you may not like me
or you may even detest me/
You may even have an agenda to constantly test me/
You may even smile in front of me and laugh at my
jokes/
Or give me compliments
and comment on the words I spoke/

Wars have been fought, won, and loss when conflicts have arisen over matters of faith. We should examine how or why another's faith threaten us? Why does their belief bother you? It's their prerogative. For the atheist, why does it concern you who, why or that I worship someone that you believe doesn't exist? Isn't that my issue? How, why or when did it become yours?

I feel there's so much you don't know about me/
So let's have a chat and by the end you'll see/
I'm as real as they come and even though a sinner/
Set free through the grace of God I have been
transformed into a winner/

Christianity isn't a belief system or faith that should ever be forced upon anyone. If that has happened then I can assure you that the person who was forcing it, wasn't practicing Christianity. When we read in the word, we see that God has given each person free will. You and I are free to choose or not. With Christ there comes liberty, not control, or forcefulness. Bottom line, I rather keep on praising HIM with my faith. I'd rather praise knowing HE does exist than to be found failing to praise HIM thinking that HE doesn't. Since most religions exist on the premise of good works, if I'm wrong (as long as I'm doing good) I will have lost nothing. On the other hand, if you are wrong you will have missed Heaven. As ministers of the Good News (Gospel) and disciples of the Great Commission it's our job to spread the Gospel. We do our best to spread the Gospel but in the end its your choice. You get to choose if you want your life to change. You get to decide if you want more. You can opt for salvation, redemption and a relationship with Christ. Why be bitter when you can be better?

Although, many times, I've failed Him,
He's never failed me/
He's freed me from sins
that have for so long derailed me/
Am I going to preach? No I prefer to testify/
I am nowhere near perfect but a lot has been
rectified...

Everyone doesn't have to like you. I may sound pretty harsh to hear, but it's true. You don't have to like any one either. However, what I've observed and witness is what various individuals dislike has done. Our dislike can result in much backstabbing, backbiting and unapologetic dialogues. Why? Because we haven't learned how to embrace differences and change.

So much has changed that it's strange to me/
But I can no longer ignore this wonderful change in me/
Some say I'm conceited but that hurts, yes it does/
Some even think that I think I'm better
but I'm better than what I was/

When you look at most successful people, what do you think made them successful? Do you think they haven't encountered conflict? I believe that what many of them have mastered is conflict. Many of them have to deal with backlash, hate, jealousy and disrespect. Yet, in spite of these attacks on their character, they never let that stop them from becoming successful.

You see since the Holy Ghost lives in me,
He gives me guidance/
No more leaning on my own understandings
since He's my greatest reliance/
This world is in turmoil and no one's trying to save it/
Such a shame especially with everything that He gave it...

Does it hurt to be called out of your name? Does it hurt to hear hateful rhetoric and opinions about who you are? Does it pain a person even more when you do your best to help others, yet they attack? Even still the fact that you never intended to hurt anyone. Absolutely. Therefore, what should you do when you experience this kind of ignorance? What should you do when others put you down and attack your character? Nothing. Yes, you heard me correctly. I said, "Do nothing."

Why am I saying this? Because I want you to be wiser, smarter and more strategic. What you need to understand is that when insults or ignorant people come against you, it's a trick. The bait is to get you to react. The trick is to get you to turn into them. Sometimes, the goal is to make you worse than them.

As I told you in the beginning of this section, they don't have to like you, and you don't have to like them. You don't have to like them. That is true. However, by God's law, you must love them. "Love thy neighbor." Kill them with kindness. Love is the only thing that exist that can diffuse hate. Hate doesn't get rid of hate. Hate only exacerbates the problem of hate. Smile through it all. Believe it or not a smile is a powerful weapon. It shows strength, power, and diligence. Forgiveness allows you to let go, and a smile is the proof that you did.

The ones who can't let things go are suffering. They are suffering mentally, emotionally, spiritually and even physically. They may be suffering more than you can imagine. Your ability to let go and let GOD frees you from a world of hurt. Your ability to forgive opens you up to receive more of God's blessings. God has blessings and opportunities made just for you. No one said it was going to be easy. However, anything worth having, is worth fighting for. You are going to have to fight for your success, deliverance and blessings. The rewards that come from faith and obedience is more than rewarding. What God has in store is awesome.

"Cards On The Table"
The truth is, you may not like me
or you may even detest me/
You may even have an agenda to constantly test me/
You may even smile in front of me and laugh at my
jokes/
Or give me compliments
and comment on the words I spoke/
I feel there's so much you don't know about me/
So let's have a chat and by the end you'll see/
I'm as real as they come and even though a sinner/
Set free through the grace of God I have been
transformed into a winner/
Although, many times, I've failed Him,

He's never failed me/

He's freed me from sins

that have for so long derailed me/

Am I going to preach? No I prefer to testify/

I am nowhere near perfect but a lot has been

rectified/

So much has changed that it's strange to me/

But I can no longer ignore this wonderful change in

me/

Some say I'm conceited but that hurts, yes it does/

Some even think that I think I'm better

but I'm better than what I was/

You see since the Holy Ghost lives in me,

He gives me guidance/

No more leaning on my own understandings

since He's my greatest reliance/

This world is in turmoil and no one's trying to save

it/

Such a shame especially with everything that He

gave it/

I identify myself as a child of the Most High/

And so much has happened that it has opened my

eyes/

I don't have to agree, nor do I have to condone/
Nor is the answer to the problem to leave it alone/
But I pray Almighty God
that You continue to have mercy
and show You're goodness/
Every time wondering if this could get any worse,
could this?/
I'm in agreement with,
"Let he who is without sin cast the first stone"/
Yes, we all have our crosses to bare
but we don't have to do it alone/
His grace is sufficient
and His love is everlasting/
His Glory should be acknowledged
more than it has been/
We serve a great God who is willing and able/
Since His Word is truth, those are my cards on the
table.

FORGIVENESS

Have you ever said something you wish you could take back? Ever said something you wish you didn't say? Have you ever done something you wish didn't do? Do you feel a sense of hopelessness, as if it's too far gone to be resolved? Do you find yourself repeating the same offense? Do you beat up on yourself for not learning from the first time you committed the offense?

Here is something to consider; no matter what you may think or say, you cannot compare your feelings to the person on the receiving end. We can't imagine the thoughts and feelings of the person we are hurting. It's so easy to add ourselves into the equation. Often we may do this to receive equal pity. We may inflate our pain, instead of accepting responsibility for the role we've played in the scenario. I understand, no one wants the blame or to admit fault. I guess accepting the blame would mean admitting wrong and who wants to do that? Who wants to pay the price of the person at fault? I've got good news for you, FORGIVENESS IS FREE. There's no cost for it.

I think about all the times I've made mistakes
but also made corrections.
I've made bad decisions
but also made some good choices.
I've done things I've regretted
and other things I'll never forget it.
I've lost some friends and made new ones.
I asked for forgiveness for the ones I've hurt
and forgave those who hurt me.
Life is too short to carry burdens.
God said, He will never leave me nor forsake me
and He didn't. He made me stronger,
wiser and proved I was worthy of love.

Forgiveness is freeing. It removes the burdens and heavy loads of guilt and suffering. Forgiveness is freedom. It allows you to walk with GOD'S grace and mercy into purpose. When you ask for forgiveness, you accept your part in the hurt you've caused. When you practice forgiveness, you remove the stress, the grudges, the frustration and the anger, so it doesn't fester into anything more.

I often ask God for forgiveness for instances where I've done things to hurt Him. What hurts God? Sin. So, I've asked Him to forgive me of any sins I've committed. I've asked my wife for forgiveness for the times I was unsupportive, insensitive or disrespectful to her feelings in any way. I've had to ask my children for forgiveness for any hurt or confusion I may have caused them. Forgiveness is a practice we must engage in daily.

Forgiveness represents submission. I believe that GOD wants us to be submissive. When we are submissive we open our heart. It's only with an open heart, mind and spirit that we can really and truly be used by HIM.

There are many things that we see as unforgivable, such as lying, stealing, cheating, abuse, rape, murder and molestation. What do you do when you are asked to forgive the unforgivable? What about those brave families? There have been countless stories of brave men and women who lost family members to horrific acts. However, because of their faith in GOD, found the strength to forgive the perpetrator. What about when Jesus forgave Judas for his betrayal towards Him? Think about and consider that Jesus forgave him despite knowing what he was going to do.

How much are you willing to forgive? Here comes our part that's easier said than done, forgive. Sometimes we get caught up in the process of forgiving. We may focus so much on forgiving that we lose out on the act of forgiveness. In other words, forgiveness is a freeing not bondage. It shouldn't be holding you down or back. It should be helping you let go.

There is power in forgiveness and that power is freedom. Without experiencing freedom found in forgiveness, we can never move forward. Without this freedom, we can never let go. Without this freedom, we can never heal. This freedom keeps us out of bondage. This freedom keeps us from carrying baggage and holding grudges. When we use the power of forgiveness, God cancels every negative power from the enemy. We stand on GOD's word. We stand with our faith in HIM knowing that the outcome is pure, uninhibited, unashamed, unapologetic freedom. Free yourself from yourself and let GOD in. Forgiveness is a gift.

"But to those of you who will listen, I say: Love your enemies, do good to those who hate you, bless those who curse you, pray for those who mistreat you."

As I was writing this, I received troubling news about a brother named, Al Middleton, who did Hemodialysis with my wife, passed away this past Wednesday at his home. We never know when it's our time, but we can start now to forgive all who hurt us and free our spirits from unneeded grief and stress. I looked forward to us meeting again and even though I'm sad that he's gone, I'm glad he knew I loved and appreciated him for all he did for me and my wife.

Listen..... the God I serve, has transformed broken men into doers of His word. He has converted murderers and thieves through the cross. He has used the least likely candidates to serve Him and preach His word. God can change anyone, even a man that spews hatred through racism, hedonism, fascism, egoism, sexism, sarcasm and bitterness.

Forgiveness doesn't mean to see the offense and pretend to accept it. Forgiveness means to release your need for revenge, get even or make the person pay. Forgiveness means to let go of your need to be right or justified in the situation. Its releasing the person and yourself from the offense. It requires abolishing and erasing the wrong done. Man, that sure isn't easy. As a matter of fact to forgive can be downright hard. However, it is a choice and its doable.

I've heard people say, "I'll forgive but I won't forget." Here is the problem with that statement. In order to forgive, you must let go and not hold on. When God forgives our sins (and we have plenty), it goes into the sea of forgetfulness. He never brings it up again. Beginning from the time we asked for our sin to be absolved God wipes the slate clean (1 John 1:9).

Remember when Jesus was on the cross imploring God to forgive those who put Him there? He asked God the Father to "forgive them, for they know not what they do?" Here is the thing, Jesus was praying for all of those who nailed Him to the cross. But I don't believe, they believe they have done anything wrong. Someone told me one day that "You can't fix stupid." Further, what if you don't know you're stupid? What happens then? How can you fix something that you don't believe needs fixing? We can't fix someone who doesn't want to be fixed, BUT GOD CAN.

I said this before, but I'll say it again because it merits repeating, forgiveness is also freeing the mind of unnecessary, unwarranted, unconscionable, unfavorable and undesirable stress. Free yourself from the monotony of diligently seeking solutions that GOD already has the remedy for. GOD hears us. He told Moses, "I have heard my people cry." Trust me, He hears us right now. Once again, let go and let GOD.

CHAPTER 10

A MAN OF GRACE WAS BORN

There are some discrepancies about being a man and being a man of God. Manhood has been stereotyped in three categories, what he can do, can't do and what he's supposed to do. There are noticeable and recognizable differences. Men are supposed to be in control. They are supposed to be fearless and courageous. We expect men to take care of everything and fix problems.

We keep hearing terms and phrases such as, "Man up!" " Be a man!" or "Act like a man!" We get questions such as, "Are you a man or a mouse?" or "What kind of a man are you?" These are just some of the attacks on manhood effecting a man's self-worth. These attacks come as a result of how the world views and defines the role of a man. On the other hand, we have who and what God calls us to be as men. A man of God and a man of Grace, fears God, Loves God, and Honors God. A man of God and Grace worships God, Praises God, and Obeys God. A man of God and Grace, doesn't know everything but takes comfort in knowing someone who does.

The enemy is pompous
and will placate the passages from God's pristine
Providence
but there can be no pleasure without pain
just like there can be no passion without pressure.

When a man fears God, he is feared by the enemy. When he loves God, he loves everyone. When he honors, worships and praises God, it's with everything in Him. And when he obeys God, he obeys Him completely without reservation.

One of the biggest misconceptions and myths we are bombarded with repeatedly is that "Men are not supposed to cry." We are expected to keep all of our emotions bottled up inside and pretend to be so strong.

However, being in control, remaining fearless, staying resourceful and fighting for survival can and will take its toll. In order for a man to hold it all together for his family and peace will work to deplete his energy and strength. Working to maintain this super hero image will build stress and frustration. The sheer act of being a man will increases fear of failure. Many men suffer from the high expectations of who he should be not being reached. In my opinion, men should cry. A man's most effective cry is crying out to Jesus.

Let Him lighten your load and burdens and give you peace. Give you understanding and wisdom and show you the design and plan of a Godly man.

A man of God and Grace serves God. He recognizes he has weaknesses and strengths. He understands that despite his shortcomings he has strength through the Son of God. A man of Grace understands that its through Christ that his real power exist. So, the question is do you want to be a man of the world or a man of God? Do you want to be a man of the world or a man of Grace? Tell the truth and free yourself from who you claim to be. Allow yourself to be who you are.

I did a self-check today. I finally realized that I'm pretty awesome just the way I am. Even if I could stand to use some improvements, SO WHAT! I never said I was perfect and who of the flesh, can? I grew up a regular kid with two sisters, one older, one younger. I grew up in a house on the corner. My best friend lived up the block. I went to elementary school down the street. I remained not the best student because I'm easily distracted. I constantly lose focus. I still don't like reading but love words, go figure.

My artistic, rap, and drawing abilities made me popular in grade school, high school and college. I loved attention that drew love and adoration but quickly realized it was a drug. The stage became an addiction from which I couldn't get enough. I loved the microphone. I loved making people laugh and feel good. Truth be told, I still do. I've bounced from college to the armed forces (medical honorable discharge) then from job to job.

Every girl I liked did not feel the same. I lived in the friend zone for a majority of my adolescence. When I finally got a girlfriend all the past rejections made me too paranoid from insecurity to keep her. As a result, I lost her and every relationship after. I blamed everyone else but myself for my failures. I became a child of divorce, a participant and later on a student of it.

I was diagnosed with depression. All of this came after the loss of my father and demise of 2 marriages. All the while, I was going through child custody issues and obesity. I became lonely and bitter. I made attempts to meet new people and had encounters with some doozies. GOD put me in alignment with my queen. We met on Myspace and I've never was happier. Besides the loss of my "wife4life," Sharon, I have my own health issues that have slowed down a lot of my activities. I've managed to complete my training and took great care of my better half for over a decade until she went on to glory.

I shared my truth to say, there were many times I could've checked myself out. Thanks, be unto God, that GOD wouldn't let me. I could've given up on love and relationships, but GOD wouldn't let me. I could've thrown in the towel with my education, but GOD wouldn't let me. I also could've held back all this truth, but GOD wouldn't let me.

The truth is no one's story is over yet. God may be waiting on us to turn to the next chapter. If you're stuck in one chapter, He'll get you through if you just be patient. While some individual's stories are longer and others are shorter, they all have meaning and purpose. Your story may help someone else. Share your truths because your truth are your testimony. Our testimonies belong to God.

The question was never what can God do for us, the question was and is what aren't we doing for God? Who can ever question or challenge the Omnipotent, the Omnipresent and the Omniscient God? Who can direct the one who sits high and looks low, the Creator of heaven and earth?

He is Jehovah Rophe, Jehovah Nissi, and Jehovah Shalom. He is our Provider, Protector, Judge and most of all Father.

The challenge is not in who He is but what are we doing to acknowledge His presence. What are we doing to thank Him for all He's done, all He's doing and all He's yet to do? What are we doing to serve Him, to worship Him, to praise him? What are we doing to spread His love, obey His word and follow His commandments? What are we doing to make His world better and stronger? How are we using kindness, generosity and love?

My brothers, what are we doing to cover our families, walk in His light and live righteously? How are you moving towards being Godly men of Grace? My sisters, what are you doing to be virtuous, holy, and strong as Godly women? Why aren't we raising more Godly children? The world is not theirs, yours or ours, it's His. We don't own anything. Everything is His. Let's honor God by showing Him how much you love and appreciate Him. Let's love one another, be kind, generous, honest, genuine and loving. God is all those things and more. Let's ask not what God can do for you, but what can you do for God.

Made in the USA
Columbia, SC
18 October 2020

23055805R00100